THE
MAGIC
OF
TURKEY

A GUIDE TO THE TURKISH COAST

ALFREDO GIACON

Foreword by Jimmy Cornell

SHERIDAN HOUSE

To my father, romantic voyager

First published 2008
in the United States of America by
Sheridan House, Inc.
145 Palisade Street
Dobbs Ferry, NY 10522
www.sheridanhouse.com

First published in Italy under the title
Magica Turchia: Guide alle coste turche
by Ugo Mursia Editore S.p.A, Milano

Library of Congress Cataloging-in-Publication Data
Giacon, Alfredo, 1961–
    [Magica Turchia. English]
    The magic of Turkey : a guide to the Turkish coast / Alfredo Giacon ;
foreword by Jimmy Cornell.
        p. cm.
    Includes index.
    ISBN 978-1-57409-270-7 (pbk. : alk. paper)
    1. Aegean Sea Coast (Turkey)—Guidebooks. 2. Boats and boating—
Turkey—Aegean Sea Coast—Guidebooks. 3. Turkey—Guidebooks.
I. Title.
    DS51.A225G5313 2008
    915.6204'4—dc22   2008048451

Photos by Alfredo Giacon
Line drawings by Giampietro Pini
Translated by Lara Fabiano
Edited by Janine Simon, Juliet Barnes
Designed by Keata Brewer

Printed in the United States of America

ISBN 918 1 57409 270 7

Adparent rari nantes in gurgite vasto, arma virum,
tabulaeque, et Troia gaza per undas.

Here and there are seen swimmers in the vast abyss,
with weapons of men, planks, and Trojan treasure
amid the waves.

Vergil, Aeneid, Book 1, Verses 118-119

Contents

JANCRIS
MIKADO 56

Ketch
Hull material: fiberglass
Deck: teak
Built in 1983 and refitted 1993
LOA: 56'
Beam: 4.85m
Draft: 2.2m
Displacement: 16 tons
Engine model: Perkins 126
Generator: 3.5 kw
Tankage: Fuel: 600L   Water: 1000L
Desalinator, waterpurifier, automatic pilot
Sails: mainsail, genoa, staysail, mizzen, 2 spinnakers
Spacious accommodations: 4 double cabins, double
stainless steel sinks with cold and hot water, large dinette,
well-equipped galley, refrigerator and freezer, chart table,
working space and roomy saloon.

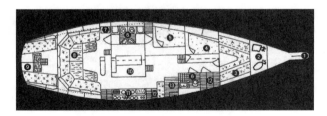

1. bowsprit/pulpit
2. sail locker
3. Front V-berth cabin
4. Double cabin
5. Double cabin with head and
   bath
6. Double cabin with shower
   (hot and cold water)
7. well-appointed navigation
   station
8. dinette with 12 seats, bar,
   stereo, CD, TV
9. crew cabin
10. engine room
11. well-equipped galley
    (3-burner stove, double
    stainless steel sinks, cold/hot
    water and sea water,
    refrigerator, freezer)
12. cupboard
13. chart table

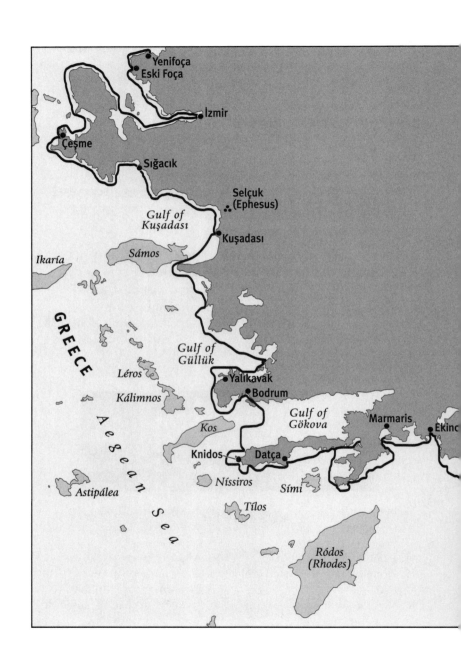

Yenifoça
Eski Foça
İzmir
Çeşme
Sığacık
Selçuk
(Ephesus)
Gulf of
Kuşadası
Kuşadası
Ikaría
Sámos
GREECE
Gulf of
Güllük
Léros
Kálimnos
Yalıkavak
Bodrum
Gulf of
Gökova
Marmaris
Ekinc
Aegean Sea
Kos
Knidos
Datça
Níssiros
Sími
Astipálea
Tílos
Ródos
(Rhodes)

N

0   20   40 miles

0   20   40 kilometers

TURKEY

Göcek

Fethiye

Antalya

Antalya
Marina

Kemer

Gulf of
Antalya

Kalkan

Finike

Kaş

Kekova

Megísti
(Kastellórizon)

M e d i t e r r a n e a n   S e a

Foreword

A small fleet of yachts gathered in the Israeli port of Ashkelon early in August 1998 for the start of the Millennium Odyssey, among them Alfredo and Nicoletta Giacon's JANCRIS. This round the world rally had a very special significance as it was meant to celebrate the start of the new millennium in a unique and original way. Participants in the Millennium Odyssey would carry a symbolic Millennium Flame around the globe and bring everywhere a message of hope and peace. The true meaning of the millennium celebrations led to the decision to have a symbolic start in Jerusalem and an equally symbolic finish in Rome—with the wide world in between.

JANCRIS was one of the first yachts to join this ambitious project after I had met Alfredo at a presentation in Italy. He immediately embraced the idea with his usual enthusiasm and, as he later told me with great excitement, JANCRIS would join the event under the auspices of the Italian cruising association CVA, thus giving many Italian sailors the opportunity to join the rally at various stages. Furthermore, Alfredo had also secured the cooperation of his home city of Padua, which he would represent during the two year long event.

One morning we left the yachts and drove to Jerusalem to the Church of the Holy Sepulchre, where the Orthodox Church, who had administered this holy place throughout its turbulent history, had agreed to put on a special ceremony for the lighting of the Millennium Lamps. These had been specially designed and each participating yacht was to carry a lamp and its flame around the world. At every stop the flame was to be handed over to local dignitaries in a special ceremony. The small fleet gradually grew to an armada of fifty yachts that over the following two years visited over forty countries in every continent, including Antarctica, the Millennium Flame, and its message, being presented to local dignitaries in all ports visited.

JANCRIS joined the larger group that sailed a warm water route that passed through the Panama Canal, South Pacific, North Indian Ocean and reached the Mediterranean via the Red Sea and Suez Canal. All along the way JANCRIS was joined by a succession of Italian sailors, who were not only enjoying the opportunity of sailing in this symbolic round the world event but were also gaining valuable offshore experience in seamanship and navigation from their accomplished hosts.

The two-year long Millennium Odyssey came to a happy ending in Rome, where Millennium Easter Monday saw a large ceremony in St Peter's Square. The Millennium Odyssey sailors had been reserved places in a special enclosure among the 100,000 pilgrims from around the world who witnessed the handing over of the Millennium Flame to Pope John Paul II.

Mission accomplished, Alfredo and Nicoletta headed east and spent the next four years visiting virtually every nook and cranny of the spectacular Turkish coast. The result of their highly enjoyable cruise is now in your hands. I hope you will share their enthusiasm for this special corner of their beloved Mediterranean.

Jimmy Cornell

Preface

It is a true privilege to sail on your own boat, free from the constraints of the calendar. When you then discover a coast that seems to have been purposefully created by Mother Nature to welcome vessels, as is the case with Turkey, you wish that the clock would stop ticking altogether.

Every nook and cranny in this country has an appeal that draws you to it. Without even noticing it, Nicoletta and I ended up spending three years living on its crystal clear waters, befriending its people, savoring its traditional cuisine with its aroma of exotic spices.

Back in Turkey with JANCRIS, near Kekova Bay

Our lifestyle changed drastically back in 1993 when we decided that it was time to break away and to live, full-time, on board our sailboat. We left the Italian coast feeling torn by our doubts and anxious about the unknown. We could not foresee what the boat and the sea would have in store; it was, after all, a totally new dimension for us.

As the days passed, JANCRIS, our wonderful sailboat, became more and more our home. Her cozy wooden interior protected us from the vagaries of the weather, and we were becoming more confident with the sea and the wind as we were gaining experience, mile after mile, maneuvering and sailing. Life at sea proved enchantingly pleasant, and everything seemed simpler and more concrete.

Our ancient Venetian maritime tradition took us eastward, to the cobalt blue Mediterranean Sea that starts its thousand-mile journey in Gibraltar and ends along the steep rugged coast of Turkey.

All our boating friends who had sailed on Turkish waters described this land with great enthusiasm—in some places a rocky desert, at times defaced by cement, but for the most part as lush and verdant as an equatorial forest, and with extraordinary archaeological treasures waiting to be discovered and admired.

How could JANCRIS' course resist the allure and the magic of the Orient?

And how do you resist the desire to discover a new land, meet a new culture and people, savor new dishes, breath in unknown fragrances?

Years and years of sailing around the labyrinth of famous and lesser-known Greek islands scattered in the Aegean Sea naturally led us onward, eastward. It was the curiosity of the traveller that guided us as we finally left the old, familiar places to explore the Turkish coast.

As we all know, people often leave their loved ones in order to satisfy the insatiable drive to discover a new horizon.

We stayed along the coast of Caria and Lycia for a few years, until 1998. Then, that year, we set sail to participate in the "Millennium Odyssey 1998-2000," an around-the-world rally organized by Jimmy Cornell to celebrate the closing of the millennium. Two years later and after more than 25,000 miles of navigation, JANCRIS returned to sail the Mediterranean Sea. After Rome, the city where the rally finished, and where we celebrated our third-place finish, we once again headed eastward, to Greece, to return to the places where a few years earlier our new life had begun. This time around, as more mature and experienced travellers, we retraced our route along the wild and bewitching coast of Turkey.

The pages of this book are not only filled with tales of our experiences; they also include practical information on all sorts of topics, ranging from anchorages and marinas and weather forecasts, to the local cuisine of one of the most fascinating coasts in the world.

The areas covered stretch from the port of Izmir to the south, southeast, up to Antalya, passing through Bodrum, Marmaris, Fethiye and Finike. With their beauty, pristine wild bays, and modern, efficient marinas, the many unforgettable spots featured in this book are sure to captivate any traveller.

We swam in crystal clear water over the submerged ruins of ancient houses; we anchored in postcard-perfect bays; moored in tiny ports unknown to most tourists; and visited legendary archaeological sites.

The temptation to describe such places and share specific up-to-date information with anyone who plans to, or simply longs to sail along the fabulous Turkish coast, is therefore hard to resist.

Yet this book should not be regarded as a complete guide to Turkey, as the tales recounted herein refer to the places to which Nicoletta and I have sailed, the towns we visited, and the friends we left behind who are always on the lookout to see whether JANCRIS' two masts reappear on the horizon.

Lush emerald green pine forests wave to the rhythm of the wind, resembling the gentle waves of a calm sea. The scent of resin, rarely perceivable when at sea, impregnates and fills the air. The reddish tufts of oleander do remind us that we are not on a mountain lake. This is Turkey! Welcome aboard JANCRIS to discover the magic of Turkey.

PART 1

The Coast of Caria: From Bodrum to Marmaris

Our Return to Turkey after the Around-The-World Rally

Berthed at the pier of the new marina of Kos, on the Greek island with the same name, JANCRIS was peacefully rocking away. The unwavering morning sun predicted another day of scorching heat, and yet it was only the beginning of May.

As the hours passed, the beautiful turquoise sky faded into what seemed a haze. After a hefty breakfast, I went on deck, while Nicoletta, below, was busy washing the cups, decorated with images of old clippers at sea. Another yawn, the last, and I cleared the mooring lines to stern that kept the boat tied to the land. Once the engine was in gear, the lines would be ready to be released into the sea. Emerging from below, Nicoletta looked around and said, "Another beautiful day," as she proceeded to stern, to the gangway.

1

Prior to any departure, there is a set of tasks that require our attention. These include removing the shore power cord from the inlet, coiling the water hose that the night before had served to fill the water tanks with 260 gallons of fresh water, and stowing it away.

A few minutes was all that JANCRIS needed to set sail. When I turned on my reliable six-cylinder Perkins Sabre engine, it started smoothly, without the slightest sign of hesitation.

With the gangway safely stowed away, the downwind line was released. A marina worker was waiting for instructions to release the dock line. We were free at last to leave the pier.

As I moved to the cockpit, I waved to Nicoletta to haul the thick rope and drop it into the water quickly. I accelerated and made headway. JANCRIS was slowly distancing herself from the two vessels she'd been moored next to and was moving ahead.

We glided smoothly on the water of the marina, not making even the smallest ripple. After we passed the breakwater, a new horizon unfolded before us, and we filled our lungs with the smell of salt water. But we could not set sail since there was not even the faintest breeze.

Just five miles along, we caught sight of our next stop, the large city of Bodrum, which that day had a dust cloud hovering above it. Bodrum would be our first stop in Turkey after four years and also where we would check in and deal with customs formalities.

The entrance to the port boasts a breathtaking view of the castle of St. Peter whose silhouette stands out from the rest of the skyline.

But the small port itself, lined with hardly visible low-rise buildings, lies obscured behind a veritable forest of the caiques' wooden masts, hundreds of them tightly moored in three rows alongside the municipal dock.

When we passed between the pontoons of the modern

marina at Bodrum, everything appeared just as it had been back in 1998.

The marina's orange "follow-me dinghy" moved full-speed toward us as we entered. Once nearby, the craft slowed down suddenly. The man steering it greeted us and told us to follow him to our already assigned place.

We docked stern-to, as usual, tying the mooring line to the bow, and then secured the stern dock lines to the floating dock. In a matter of minutes, the engine was off.

As Nicoletta was mounting the fenders, I said, "There's no doubt that there are many more boats berthed here than there were a few years ago."

"True," she replied, looking around, "but it's still a fascinating and peaceful place to visit since the marina's only a short walk from the heart of the historic town center." She added, smiling, "I still remember its hundreds of shop windows, the carpets and fake designers' clothing, and the many tourists that walked along its winding roads."

When the sun lost some intensity, I decided to go to the marina office and fill out the transit log. Valid for six months, the document lets you cruise Turkish waters without any hassles.

Air conditioning inside the office made the place pleasantly cool. I found out that I could either pay fifty dollars to an agency to handle the application or I could take care of filling out the forms personally.

With time on our hands, and as the port's customs office was nearby, we chose the money-saving option and dealt with all the formalities ourselves. In a few hours, the visa we needed was in our passports and JANCRIS was free to sail on Turkish waters.

"We can use our extra fifty dollars to dine out," I suggested to Nicoletta as we made our way back to the boat, strolling in the shadow of palm trees as they swayed above the flowerbeds.

"A wonderful idea!" she said, smiling. "I really feel like

eating a *pide* again, the ones that are cooked in the wood-burning ovens."

The pide is Italian pizza's one true rival. By no means an imitation, it is an ancient, popular native Turkish dish. Pide looks similar to pizza except for its oval shape, but instead of using mozzarella, it features another delicious local cheese variety. It is both tasty and extremely affordable.

As we passed through the entry gates to the marina and strolled along in the pedestrian area, I remarked to Nicoletta, "It's nice to be back in Turkey. It has such a different atmosphere from Greece, even if it is only a few miles away. Turkey has an Oriental feel, with an underlying passion and energy for trade and craftsmanship that the Western world has lost. The minarets with their muezzins' calls to prayer blend into a single perfect harmony with the white buildings and the city noises. Europe, which they are so eager to join, seems very far away!"

Moving her hand to clasp mine, Nicoletta said, "We'd better enjoy this land and its people without being overly concerned about what might happen in the future. This country is magnificent and we have some great memories of its landscapes. It will be nice to set sail and leave the dusty city behind as soon as possible to spend a few days in a bay. Remember the beautiful anchorage at Knidos?" Without even waiting for my reply she added, "Well, it's pide tonight, and tomorrow we head off to the south, and if we're lucky, we may even have a meltemi breeze at our back."

The sinking sun in the west set the clear sky ablaze, while eastward the earth was covered in darkness. Nicoletta emerged from below deck. Dressed for dinner, she joined me as I was sitting in the cockpit with my eyes closed, in a sort of trance, holding a glass of beer. From the speakers in the cockpit came the mellow music of Costes, the volume set low, to drown out the noise of the nearby city except for the muezzin's call to prayer. Its melancholy chant pierced the air and wailed above the melody we were listening to.

It's fantastic, I thought to myself. I kept my eyes closed, and as the noise of the cars disappeared, the stillness in the air took me a few years back when JANCRIS was anchored in Port Sudan near our friend Josko's boat, in the heart of the Red Sea.

Having crossed the Indian Ocean, which was a truly enjoyable experience, we had stopped in Djibouti and were bound northward. We figured that our navigation would be extremely tough: with constant contrary winds and notorious high waves that often reduced to smithereens any vessel that obstinately attempted to oppose them. In fact, the miles we covered on average, per day, had dropped drastically: in the ocean we had covered 180 miles a day, while in the Red Sea, due to the harsh sailing conditions, we travelled less than half that distance.

Luckily, a stopover was planned in Port Sudan. We would meet a dear friend, Josko, whom we had not seen for a couple of years, since the summer of 1998. We had met in Kastellorizon, and there we'd scheduled an incredible appointment for the future: to meet, at the end of March in the year 2000, at Port Sudan. And that is exactly what happened.

The muezzin's call to prayer in Bodrum brought back memories of Suez, where, on the morning of April 4, we were anchored in front of the yacht club, anxiously awaiting the moment we would begin crossing the famous canal to reach the Mediterranean and complete our circumnavigation with the Millennium Odyssey.

When I opened my eyes to sip my beer, Nicoletta was standing before me like a blonde mermaid, with her fair, lightly tanned complexion; she stared at me with her big blue eyes and asked, "Are you OK?"

"Never better," I replied. "The atmosphere brought

back memories of the Red Sea. Let's go. We have a long walk ahead of us."

The old city of Bodrum changes atmosphere in the evening: darkness swallows the heat, the dust, and the sweaty people. A refreshing breeze sweeps across a multiracial crowd of tourists and the multicolored neon lights of thousands of shops and restaurants.

Music, a mix of modern and folk, resounds as you come out of shops and onto the streets, marking a dichotomy of styles that is also reflected in the array of goods displayed in shop windows. Colorful wool carpets and kilim shops stand next to brightly lit stores that offer precious looking watches like Rolex, Cartier and other brands, all fake. Clothing shops and small boutiques sell handicrafts like beautiful pipes and reproductions of old Byzantine ceramic ware.

All over town, as the place is a tourist trap, the words "Yes, please" echo in your ears as you pass by stores and restaurants. Then, young boys, who overhear the few words tourists utter, generally address them in their language. For the most part, these talented hawkers are not annoyingly aggressive, and, when you see them in action, they're actually quite smooth.

Leaving the small but luxurious shopping area behind the pontoons of the marina, we walked along the municipal dock, where hundreds of caiques, the famous, traditional pine Turkish sailing vessels, all stacked up, are berthed. From afar, some evoke images of ancient pirate ships that were characterized by sterncastles and large windows aft. Others, very large ones, look like transoceanic clippers, though they do not perform well under sail. The caiques are an integral part of the general Turkish panorama, and it is rare to find a bay without them.

On our way to the historic town center, specifically to the pedestrian area, Nicoletta decided to detour onto a narrow, crowded, winding backstreet. In a matter of seconds we were plunged into the heart of the former old fishermen's village of Bodrum, which is now packed with stores for tourists.

The backstreet soon widened and opened onto a Venetian-style square that had a couple of restaurants and a pizzeria, or I should call it a pideria? Just our place! Though there weren't many tables in the little square, one was free, and we immediately occupied it. "Only tourists eat at this hour; Turks start eating after 10 p.m. and this place caters mostly to locals," said Nicoletta as she looked through the menu a young boy had brought. The menu was a sheet that was folded in two with nine pictures representing the different pide, and their prices, which never exceeded five dollars, next to the images.

Moving closer to Nicoletta, who had already chosen her dish, I said, "Menus with pictures are a great way to know what you are ordering."

"I'll have a pide with tomatoes, cheese, and ground beef with an egg on top," she said, beaming with a look denoting that she was challenging me.

"So much for dieting. So you are challenging me? Then I'll have the same plus a few thin slices of sweet green pepper on top," I replied, amused.

"To digest it all and call it a night we can go for a stroll and window shopping," she added, even more cheerfully.

Knidos: Harmony restored

"Head-to-wind!" I called out to Nicoletta from the cockpit. And she hoisted the mizzen sail. For a few seconds the white Dacron whipped violently in the air as the last inches of the halyards were hauled in tight, taming the rebellious sail.

Nicoletta eased the sheet and I bore up to get JANCRIS moving on course. With a little genoa unfurled, JANCRIS glided south, leaving the port of Bodrum behind.

"With 28 knots of apparent wind," I announced to Nicoletta who looked at me perplexed, "we are sailing at nine knots so there must be more than thirty knots of wind; luckily the sea is calm and the wind is abaft. The rudder is not under pressure and the boat is well balanced. I'll put the autopilot on so I can go chart the missing mile," I added, leaving the steering wheel.

With the high mountains of the island of Kos, the real wind increased, and though we were navigating a few miles from there, violent gusts brought the salty white foam of unruly waves splashing onto the teak deck, glazing it with a beautiful gold glitter.

As we got closer to Cape Krio (*Deveboynu Burnu*, in Turkish), and Kos grew smaller and smaller, the stormy wind turned into a breeze. We were able to release the genoa completely for maximum wind exposure. The wind, though very light, filled the sail, and its radiant colors shone under the strong Aegean sun.

The cobalt blue sea was more than three hundred feet deep; incredibly, we were just a few feet from the tall rocky cliff where a beautiful lighthouse is perched.

Since there was no wind at all, and another mile to go, in order to round the cape we had to haul down the two sails that had quickly brought us to our destination.

The bay offered a pristine beauty that had remained un-altered over the centuries. There were with no busy roads or villages around, only the striking ruins of an ancient Greek city and its theater.

"We could drop the anchor over toward the tiny beach, on the right," Nicoletta proposed as she headed to the bow to prepare the anchor. She stopped and added, "Remember the last time we were here a few years ago? There was a strong wind, and our anchor dragged so we needed a number of attempts to finally cast it in the 'right' bottom where there was no sea grass. I'm sure that spot is somewhere on the right."

She then pointed to the end of the bay where the water was lighter in color, a turquoise hue, meaning that there was a sandy bottom, and therefore an ideal seafloor for our 66-pound Bruce anchor.

"Move ahead just a couple more feet and we are above the sand," she said from the prow, and then raised her arm.

I got into reverse gear so Nicoletta could ease the anchor down about 80 feet. A "thumbs-up" is her way of telling me that the heavy chain is taut and the anchor is holding. Before completing the maneuver, she released another 60 feet of chain into the water, for a total of more than 140. (In the Mediterranean, safe anchoring requires more chain than is normally used in the waters of the U.S. eastern seaboard where we sailed, as the bottom is not always a good holding ground.)

The wind settled at about 15 knots leaving the sky a crisp blue without a cloud in sight. The wind didn't bother us—we had mounted a wind generator halfway up the mizzenmast to fully charge the batteries on board: two for the main engine and four dedicated to service.

"The Turks won't mind if we eat a tasty Greek salad topped with a big chunk of feta cheese—that cheese we bought in Kos and kept in the refrigerator for a while," said Nicoletta from the cockpit where she'd found shelter from the sun under the bimini.

"Surely not," I replied merrily, "especially since I am so hungry that I could take a bite out of somebody," and I dashed toward her to nibble her warm, sun-splashed shoulder.

JANCRIS, and the few other boats moored in the bay, danced in the spring wind. On land, the thorny vegetation and the olive trees, bent over the years by the wind, dotted the landscape with their green hues; the sun-baked brushwood took on a hay-colored sheen that lingered all summer long.

The hills, on which the flourishing Greek city once stood, gently emerged from the sea. I could not help but wonder how chaotic it must have been, five hundred years before Christ, to moor at Knidos, a famous maritime power of the Aegean Sea.

I contemplated its small theater that sits by the sea and the foundations of some of the buildings, and a little further up I detected the remains of yet another Greek theater. I had visited that one a few years earlier, as I was exploring the area. I was awestruck and mystified by the way these remains lay around in a timeless clutter, to witness the succession of civilizations. The ancient city stood on the tip of a long, narrow peninsula that protrudes westward, as if it were challenging the other shore of the Mediterranean. Centuries and centuries ago, it harbored vessels all year round in two different ports: the summer port, which protected ships from the predominant northerly wind and the winter port, which sheltered them from the southerly wind.

The wind kept blowing, but fortunately, the afternoon gusts brought relief to our sun-drenched skin. I suggested to Nicoletta, who was sipping her coffee, "Since the heat is no longer unbearable, why don't we go ashore?"

"Great idea, that will give us plenty of time to visit the archaeological site," and she added, "Since we were last here, it looks like the excavations have gone on. This site truly deserves to be explored because it is likely that more archaeological treasures will be found."

Our beautiful white inflatable fiberglass-bottom Arimar dinghy was tied to stern. Its 15 hp Yamaha outboard was ready to take us speedily ashore to the makeshift pontoon of an abandoned restaurant that was set on the beach toward the end of the bay.

"Didn't we dine at this restaurant?" I asked Nicoletta, and then I immediately recalled, "We had grilled bass kebabs with fries. They were truly delicious! But may be it is best that it closed down. It is rather absurd to have a restaurant inside an archaeological site, in a context like this."

Nicoletta agreed with a nod.

In the meantime, the dinghy's keel ran smoothly into the sand as we reached the shore.

I preferred to head straight toward the beach to get off the tender since the pile of twisted rusty iron that served as the pontoon's frame did not seem solid enough.

With the cool seawater reaching our ankles, Nicoletta, who was standing on the left, and I on the right, took the tender by its side handles and hoisted it a few feet up to reposition it on shore. In no time at all, a Turk, with a mustache and a smile, came toward us to tell us this was an archaeological site and we therefore had to pay for an entry ticket. His heavy arm, hidden in part by the rolled up sleeve of his creamy shirt, pointed toward a kiosk where the tickets were sold. The man followed us as we headed in that direction. In a split second he slipped inside the kiosk, put an official looking hat on, and sat down on a white plastic chair to tear out our two tickets from a block.

"Ten dollars!" he said, handing us the tickets.

"How can we be sure that we have to pay?" asked Nicoletta, raising a good point.

"The tickets seem like regular tickets; they're like the ones we bought at the museum of Bodrum." With the tickets in my hand, I went on ahead and told her to pay since she had the money with her.

We walked uphill to the ruins, and every now and again we turned around to admire the view. The higher we got, the more breathtaking the panorama became, the blues of the sky fusing with the sea.

Feeling the heat, we finally sat down in the old theater on a white stone armchair that, ages ago, craftsmen had carved into a comfortable seat, complete with anatomic backrest. Our top row seats at the Greek theater towered over the bay that hosted JANCRIS.

On the hilltop, the wind carried the rustling of the foliage, and the never-ending songs of crickets and birds.

But not a human voice came from the streets—no roaring of engines, no foul smell of motor or exhaust fumes—only nature and her sounds carrying the fragrance of the late spring air. Without saying a word, and comfortably seated on the ancient artifact, we stayed motionless. Our eyes beheld the panorama and our lungs absorbed the fresh, clean air while we listened to the tales the wind carried.

A sense of total relaxation swept over us for a few minutes, or a few hours—it is unimportant. Time, in moments like this, acquires a new meaning, and, I would even say, a different dimension that allows contentment, a sense of satisfaction, regardless of duration. The secret is not to interrupt this harmonious balance since it dissolves on its own, at the right time. And when this happens, and you regain your faculties, you realize that something extraordinary has happened, a sort of miracle!

A similar sensation overtook me in the middle of the Indian Ocean, during a crossing. A week had gone by since we had left the atolls of the Maldives. The two of us, Nicoletta and I, had many more days of navigation ahead of us before we would reach our destination, Djibouti.

With the monsoon blowing steadily, as it had for days, neither gusting violently nor subsiding, JANCRIS danced briskly on the waves with her sails well balanced. I was steering her, and Nicoletta, who had finished her shift at the wheel, was resting in the cabin.

It was the middle of the night, and a full moon shone, ridding the night of its oppressive darkness. A patina shone on every visible object, including the sea, whose perpetual motion seemed made of liquid silver.

So spectacular was the atmosphere, that I decided I would set the automatic pilot and sit on the small bench astern to absorb nature's wonders. The wake left by JANCRIS sparkled on the water and the starry sky shone above me.

I felt as though I were onboard a spaceship travelling

past planets, asteroids and stars, in an eternal astral silence, light years away from everything and everyone, zigzagging my craft through the perils of the cosmos.

And this, indeed, is exactly what we did that night on the ocean: we danced to avoid obstacles, to soften the impact of the waves, to strike a perfect harmony between the wind, the sea and the boat. We were sailing thousands of miles from the nearest city, far from people, cars, from chaos, malice or war. Alas, faraway, too, was the warmth of my loved ones, that human kindness capable of disarming even the most cynical among us.

That night, the world around me sparked such a feeling of awe in me that I lost all sense of time.

All my senses alert, I was making sure I would pick up the slightest signal of danger to us or our boat, but the minutes and the hours ticked away so quickly that when my shift was over I did not wake Nicoletta. I stayed on until the end, to enjoy the magic of that night.

At dawn, back in the cockpit, I was at the wheel when Nicoletta peeped in with her "Good morning." Seeing that her eyes were still half shut, and that she had to hold onto the staircase not to fall and lose her equilibrium I said, "Go back to bed . . . sleep a little more, I'm not at all tired. Actually, I'm full of energy and super awake," and so she did.

Indeed, I felt no fatigue at all and the idyll of that night was still alive in me. It energized me to such an extent that the urge to rest simply disappeared. What remained was a new, vivid desire to seek emotional truth in this unforgettable ocean.

Our Paradise

Keci Buku is a small and verdant bay located in the southern part of the Datça peninsula.

The first time we anchored there was in April of 1995. Two Italian friends of ours from the city of Padua, Lucia and Silvano, were there with their boat CHRISTINA. Expert cruisers, they are very fond of and know a great deal about the Turkish coast.

All winter long, we had left our boat in the small, dusty shipyard in Rhodes, the only one on the island.

The yard was run by a pleasant Frenchman named Gilles. He brought his personal touch to his "boat park" which over the years became a rendezvous spot for many travellers. They gravitate here, in the rainy winter season, to leave their boats on land for repair or for maintenance, and also to share their time and experience with other sailors. Rhodes is in a strategic position: it is only a few miles from the Turkish coast; it is well served by planes and ferry connections; and the shipyard is only a short distance from the fascinating medieval town.

These advantages, along with reasonable rates, were the reasons we left JANCRIS there, in the custody of Gilles, four winters in a row, and each time it was a positive experience.

In early March 1995, we were getting the boat ready to go back into the water. We had always spent a few weeks at the yard taking care of the chores to get JANCRIS ready for her launching. The place became a sort of extended family where everyone got to know each other since everyone lived on the hard, onboard their crafts. Lucia and Silvano had been living on their boat for fifteen years.

Nicoletta and I were truly surprised to hear their travel tales, in which they recounted their years of sailing around Greece and Turkey alone, never seeking any other more exotic destination. Turkey had captivated them, so they had stayed nine months, living in close contact with the local population, especially in their two favorite bays, Keci Buku and Yedi Adalari. Removed from any sort of popular tourist circuit, they enjoyed befriending the local inhabitants, and this fact, and their charm, earned them their nicknames, Fatma and Alì.

Silvano never missed an opportunity to tell us about the beauty of these bays, of how wonderful it would be to spend time together there on our boats, to do any maintenance work in such a peaceful, unpretentious setting, a place where the true Turkey reveals itself.

On very short notice, our plans suddenly changed. Nicoletta and I left Rhodes in their company and sailed toward the Turkish coast. A new hot summer season awaited us.

JANCRIS, as it is longer than CHRISTINA, was faster, so after just a few miles, we reduced the sails to adjust our pace to theirs. The roughly 28 miles of sea proved to be easy cruising thanks to great weather and wind conditions that prevailed.

The enormous and seemingly boundless gulf resembles a Norwegian fjord. It boasts many safe anchorage spots set in a landscape of remarkable beauty that, because it is so utterly appealing and safe, tempts seafarers to moor there for extended periods.

At the end of the gulf, on the southern side, there was a narrow bay, of about a half a mile. We steered JANCRIS' bow toward the little inlet. Its exquisite beauty left us awestruck. The rolling hills were blanketed with an emerald green pine forest interspersed with square or rectangular deforested patches that gleamed under the sun's rays. As green as a lake and just as still, the surface of the seawater was flat, without the slightest ripple.

In the distance, we could barely see some smoke rising up from a few white smokestacks, well hidden by the luxuriant vegetation.

Bound southward, we doubled a tiny rocky island that housed the ruins of a small Byzantine fort, and reached a short wooden pontoon where we moored.

We did not need our anchors since there were mooring buoys, and the two waiters from the little restaurant called

Iskele, located just behind the quay, secured the stern lines. They helped us tie them to the specially set solid iron rings.

The kind and very eager waiters wore what must have been their uniform: each had blue pants, a white shirt, and a strawberry red vest with a bow tie around the neck.

They were extremely careful about not getting their flashy uniforms dirty, so they handled the lines with the utmost care, trying not to splash any seawater onto their clothes. When our mooring maneuvers were over, Nicoletta looked at the waiters, amused, and then exchanged glances with me, knowing I had understood. I nodded, smiling.

CHRISTINA was moored nearby, and as I turned toward Silvano, I noticed that a small crowd had gathered around the quay, just at their stern. A stout man, who I guessed was the restaurant owner, a few of "our" waiters' colleagues, and a number of other people who had been seated at the restaurant, had gathered around to wait for Fatma and Alì to get off their boat. After many months, they were all visibly pleased and excited to see their good friends Lucia and Silvano. We too had joined the welcoming crowd that had spontaneously swarmed around our friends to celebrate their return to Turkey after a long winter break.

I stood on deck and looked around. What a stunning place! The wind was a mere breeze and not a sound disrupted the peace that reigned all around us.

The solid wooden pontoon built by the restaurant owner could hold seven or maybe eight boats, though at that time our two vessels were the only ones moored there.

A few small pilings were available for fresh water and electric energy.

Clean, totally peaceful, and nestled in a natural setting that was simply stupendous, "it's much nicer here than in any marina," I said to Silvano, who was heading my way to see whether everything was okay.

He replied, "And everything is free: the mooring, the water and the power," adding, "as long as we dine at our friend Izmed's restaurant. Believe me, even if we stayed on for two or three months, I am sure he would be happy to have us. It's no problem, it is how things are here."

"Great," I said, "then tonight we will go to Izmed's to get ripped off, and I'll order the same thing you do since you are at home here and know the house specialties."

"We'll spend less than you can imagine for dinner tonight," he laughingly reassured me, walking away with a wave of his hand.

Indeed, that night, after we'd had a delicious dinner, seated at a table that stood a few feet from the sea, the waiters in red handed us a bill that amounted to seven dollars per person, a very acceptable price even back in 1995.

It was astonishing how quickly and peacefully the days passed. The maintenance work, such as varnishing and polishing our boats to prepare the vessels for the beginning of the season, alternated with walks in the countryside, along the fertile farmland that stretched from behind the restaurant toward the village of Orhanie.

Villagers there tried selling us, for nickels and dimes, the organic seasonal produce they grew in their fields.

Fruit was handled differently: we were given a plastic bag in which we placed the fruit we picked from the trees. It was then weighed to see how much we had to pay. Everything was excellent, from the honey to the butter, the milk, the eggs, and even the chicken: that corner of paradise offered all we could wish for to fill our pantry.

One day, we took out the folding bikes that we had stowed away onboard, and rode toward the falls of Turgut. The site was in the midst of a pine and birch forest, only a few miles from our mooring spot, in the mountains. The paved road at a certain point became a dirt road. It sloped gently uphill at first, but eventually became so steep that we had to dismount and proceed on foot. The farther on we moved, the craggier the conditions of the road, and it then turned into a path, with sparkling, lively brooks crossing it.

Silvano strode ahead, sure-footed, closely followed by Lucia; we, on the other hand, were less convinced that the exhausting climb would be repaid by the beauty of the falls that Silvano had described with so much enthusiasm.

Out of the blue, the roaring of an engine shattered the quiet of nature that had surrounded us. The four of us all turned back and saw a few yellow convertible Jeeps packed with tourists, dashing and swerving around large rocks, spewing dense clouds of black exhaust fumes. They drove past us, waving, and then disappeared into the dark forest. Silvano looked as if he had received a sudden unexpected blow.

"Did you see that?" he exclaimed once he recovered from the shock, "Now they get here with Jeeps and soon, they'll be coming even with buses, as long as the roads are repaired a little. Did you see that!"

"Don't take it so much to heart, Silvano," I said, catching up to him, "Nature here is too wild to be destroyed by man. But how much further is it? My legs are getting stiff and I don't even want to think about going back."

As he continued his ascent he said, "We're almost there. Be prepared for the breathtaking show."

Soon after, thankfully, we reached a large clearing shaded by a canopy of tall trees. There were also some small stone and mud dwellings. Brooks gurgled and flowed next to them, while further up, amid the trees, I noticed a makeshift wooden parapet, and the tourists who had just passed us, leaning over it.

We parked the bicycles and continued on foot, fortified by the refreshing, cool air of the forest. From the small village, a dirt pathway wound its way around broad tree trunks and huge gray rocks covered with dark moss.

Once we reached the wooden fence, the dirt road was covered with wooden boards on which some tables and wicker chairs had been arranged. Against a smoke-blackened stone wall appeared a primitive fireplace and an elderly woman, dressed in black, stooping to cook a sort of flat bread, like tortillas, over the fire.

"They are called *borek*," said Lucia, surprised to see the tiny improvised restaurant. "They pour a batter onto a hot pan, which, when ready, is topped with goat cheese and a mixture of local herbs, cooked and then rolled. It is delicious. At times you even find smaller ones that are fried."

"It must be the fresh air or the walk, but I'm really hungry . . ."

"I'd prefer to go see the falls first. Then we could come back here to eat and drink," I said, interrupting Nicoletta who approved without comment.

A marked path fringed the brook and led to peaceful lakelets of crystal clear water that had formed along the flatter areas. These alternated with waterfalls of different sizes, whose crashing echo could be heard for yards in the forest. While ascending, several times I noticed the still profile of a trout camouflaged amid the pebbly bottom, or hidden under a birch branch that stuck out over the water, ready to prey on its victims. All of a sudden, the uphill hike became so steep that we had to climb up the slope, while the rumble of water overwhelmed all other sounds in the forest. The closer we got to the source of the sound, the more the air smelled of mold and humidity. Silvano had to yell to be heard, and still his voice was hardly audible, though he was just a few feet from me. An indistinct landscape, recalling the enchanted woods of fairytales, emerged from a cloud of mist sprayed by the waterfall, which plunged powerfully down thirty feet into a glassy pool that reflected the green tones of the forest crown. All around, tall grasses thrived between enormous polished granite boulders, and knotty, old, partially rotted tree trunks seemed to reach toward the sky in bizarre forms and curves.

Some northern European tourists could be heard shrieking as they dove from the top of the cascade into the pool.

Attracted by the idea of diving in myself, I dipped my

foot in the water to test its temperature. Having come directly from the inland mountains that were still blanketed in snow, the water literally froze my leg, numbing it up to my knee. None of us dreamt of jumping into the transparent freezing cold water. So, we decided to reverse our course and head back to the valley to eat one of those warm *boreks* made by the old woman.

Total Freedom

"Down with the sails," suggested Nicoletta as we reached Cape Karaburun. "After rounding the cape, we could run into some challenging, gusty winds. Two miles are all we need to reach our destination, so there is no rush. Let's leave only the mainsail—it will help maintain our speed."

We did just that, and in a few minutes JANCRIS glided on the blue water swept by the violent wind coming from the nearby rocky hills.

As we approached the entry of the large bay, we wondered if things had changed since we were last there, back in 1998.

After five years of absence we rounded the bay's imaginary entry line where, for many years in a row, we had anchored for at least a week. And where an old friend might be still waiting for us.

"It looks as if nothing has changed," said Nicoletta, "then again, in a rugged, rocky area like this, what can you expect them to build here? There isn't even a road."

In fact, all did seem unaltered, until we moved further along a small promontory, and I spotted Mustafà's little restaurant, a small stone house with a pergola just by the beach.

Nicoletta, who was at the bow preparing a line to secure it to the mooring buoy, also noticed that something had changed.

Making her way to the helm she said, confused, "There's a new wooden pontoon that I do not recall seeing before. But the orange mooring buoys are still there. I don't know what to do. In the past, Mustafà's brother, on his wooden boat in the middle of the bay, would be there to direct us and tell us which buoy to use."

Just as she finished her sentence, the old rowing boat we were used to seeing did approach us, but this time with a pretty young girl onboard who was rowing full speed.

When she was close enough for us to hear her, she told us that we must use an inner buoy, the one that was close to the promontory. She then moved toward the buoy and passed it to Nicoletta.

I proceeded with the mooring maneuver and hauled the stern line to another girl, older and taller, who was standing on land. She deftly took the windward rope and tied it to a ring on the wooden pontoon built of thick boards.

Nicoletta, after having secured the mooring buoy to the bow, came to stern with the other mooring line and the gangway.

When the gangway was safely put down, Mustafà arrived. Striding toward us with his arms wide open, he gave us a big smile, revealing his set of black rotting incisors.

"Hey buddy, great to see you and your beautiful wife. How many years has it been?" He asked in his broken English, "four or no, five maybe."

"Right, five," I answered and got off the boat to hug him.

After greeting Nicoletta and me, he rounded up his family on the dock.

The wife, whom I remembered as a pleasant looking girl, was now a stout woman. She had changed remarkably over the years we were absent. Now she was affectionately wrapped around her husband's right arm. On his left, Mustafà proudly pointed to three lovely girls; two of them were the girls who had helped us moor—the middle child had been paddling the boat, while the eldest helped us dock and collect the lines. Smiling, the girls lined up according to their ages and moved our way, with their hands outstretched, ready to greet us.

"Your girls are gorgeous," said Nicoletta. "We only remember seeing two daughters before leaving on our round-the-world tour, and they were very young."

"When you left, my wife was already expecting our third child," he said, continuing to smile jovially. I am sure that his smile was the same one he wore when he first spotted JANCRIS in the distance. He then added, "In the hopes of having a son, we tried again, and here I am surrounded by four women. Who would have ever thought!"

We talked for hours, but the hot afternoon sun was baking our skin and so we decided to say goodbye and get back to our chores. Before going onboard, however, Nicoletta chose to do what the young girls had done a little earlier, run along the dock and dive into the sea. When her head reappeared above the surface, she invited me along, saying, "Come on, the water is just perfect," and before swimming away she added, "Come swim and I promise to help you with the boating chores and the tidying up."

She didn't have to ask me twice. I ran and "splash!"

Later that evening we dined at Mustafà's. Plenty of tables and white plastic chairs were set under the pergola, and the gray cement floor was covered with colorful mats that local village women had crafted during the winter. Electric power was supplied by the old generator behind the house, enclosed in a soundproof room.

The electric generator assures that beer can be served ice cold, that food can be refrigerated and kept fresh, and that the premises have light. In fact, from the sea, the warm amber light seems more like the flame of an oil lamp rather than its less romantic counterpart, the lightbulb. Water is pumped from an underground source. In the middle of nowhere, Mustafà offers proper and pleasant service to those who seek the tranquility of a deserted and pristine bay, with the option of either spending the evening aboard or dining out in his restaurant, whether it's just for a cool beer or to savor the homemade traditional cuisine cooked by his wife.

Being our friend, he arranged a special table for us, a little out-of-the-way from the rest, which overlooked the reef and the sea beneath, and was protected by a small bamboo canopy.

When we took our seats, we noticed the way the light of the small tavern spread into the surrounding darkness. The play of shadows made the rocks appear round and smooth; the sea below us glittered, enveloped in the distance by the total darkness that wrapped the entire bay. As light as the air, without the slightest noise, the youngest of the three daughters appeared. We smiled at her as she placed a candle at the center of the table. Mustafà's wife was standing by the big fire not far from where we were seated. She took out the loaves of smoking hot bread and then placed a couple of large iron pots on the fire to cook our two big fish. The scent of freshly baked bread immediately filled the air all around us. It was irresistible even to those sitting at the other tables. The guests there, like us, came from other yachts, the only way that this amazing location can be reached. Shortly after, the little girl returned with a basket full of warm bread in one hand, and cutlery in the other.

Cool Efes beer and some vegetables were our starter; the main course would be a delicious dish called *buglamà* made with grouper. It resembles the grouper dish commonly cooked in tinfoil, accompanied by vegetables and potatoes, but its unique taste and scent comes from the way it is cooked, slowly, over a wood flame.

That night our dinner was Mustafà's treat. However, in other circumstances, the cost does not exceed thirty dollars per person, including Turkish coffee and *raki*, a traditional liquor that tastes very much like anise, or like its Greek counterpart, *ouzo*.

As we had planned the night before, we left the boat moored at Mustafà's dock in the morning and went for a walk to visit the ancient megalithic walls that loom above, visible from afar. We had seen them from the boat as we were entering the bay.

"Are you sure you don't want to use the dinghy to get a little closer?" was the question that Nicoletta kept asking over and over again, adding, "It will get us there much faster, and that way, we don't even risk scraping our knees on thorny hedges the way we did years ago."

"Go on, keep walking, Lazy Bones. After what we ate last night, a long, beautiful walk will do us good."

It is not relaxing to hike among all the stones, trying not to trip over anything. Actually, the easiest way to cross this local terrain is to follow the red dirt track traced by herds of goats. They seem perfectly at ease in this habitat and always manage to avoid the rocks and thorny hedges. Keeping our gaze constantly focused on the ground to avoid any obstacles, we end up missing out on the surrounding natural beauty. So with the excuse of catching our breath, we stopped from time to time to lift our gaze and take in the fresh, pure air. At the same time, we had a chance to admire the marvelous view.

Often, you spend more time than you expect entranced by the sheer beauty of these untouched, rugged, and forgotten parts of Turkey, where not a tree is in sight, and where as far as the eye can see, the land is strewn with rocks and Mediterranean vegetation emanating a scent of myrtle and oregano. Above, the cloudless spring sky is always a turquoise blue; below, the transparent, clean cobalt seawater is the same as it must have been centuries ago, when the valley, which is shaped like an amphitheater, was inhabited by hundreds of people. The many layers of terracing set into the steep hills for growing fruits and vegetables, are proof that this area was once populated. And in the background, a mountain chain blends with the overhanging sky.

Out of nowhere, from the direction of a nearby shrub, a sudden noise caught our attention. Nicoletta sprang up and landed on a rock; I, instead, stood perfectly still, and nervously observed the shrub to see what animal could have caused such a stir as it left the safe shelter of the thorny dry underbrush.

"Alfredo, get away from there; it could be a snake," whispered Nicoletta, worried.

Before I had a chance to answer, a lovely land turtle emerged into the open, advancing unabashed like an armored tank. It had quite a large shell, with beautiful colors ranging from intense tones of green to yellow; its scaly head poked out, close enough to brush my foot without even deigning to look at me. Nicoletta, who was curious, came back down from the rock and went toward the turtle, which stopped and pulled its head in, making it disappear for a moment. Then it proceeded on its march and headed noisily into another olive green patch of vegetation.

The deserted bay of Serge Limani, well-sheltered from the prevalent summer winds

Walls of a very well preserved Venetian castle, built by the Knights of Saint John

"A nice surprise, don't you think?" I asked Nicoletta who kept looking in the direction where the turtle disappeared. "Honestly, I never would have thought that this place had wild turtles; it seems more like a desert. It is very striking to see that it is vastly populated by predatory birds, hares, mice, goats and turtles," she remarked, hopping nimbly from rock to rock.

The top of the wall assures a breathtaking panorama. On clear days, the view stretches to encompass the island of Rhodes, about ten miles distant, and the sea, with its unforgettable varied blue hues, which extends to the ragged coast of Cape Karaburun. The bay seen from above reveals another three or four beautiful spots that are ideal for anchoring.

The omnipresent wind whipped the red Turkish flag that was tied to a wooden post planted on the outermost point of the bay's entrance, right in front of huge squared-off stone blocks that stood there for centuries, silent witnesses to the evolution of human events.

Sitting on one of these slabs, we watched a sailboat, which was coming from the south, lower her white sails and enter slowly, with caution, into the bay.

"From up here the boat seems so small that it looks like a nutshell," Nicoletta said. "It amazes me to think that on board such a shell we have crossed three oceans, defying waves as tall as hills and covering enormous distances sailing for weeks on end. . . . It almost seems impossible."

"And yet we did it," I said with a gleam in my eye. "We have seen the picturesque atolls of Polynesia; rocky, abandoned islands like the Galápagos; beaches as white as flour, fringed with the sinuous palm trees of the vast Australian coral reef; we have sailed amid the skyscrapers of Singapore, and have anchored right in front of the African desert on the Red Sea. *Our home* has always accompanied us everywhere. It has allowed us to sleep in our own beds and eat off our own dishes no matter where we were. It is part of our dearest memories. It is only thanks to a shell like that," I went on, indicating the small boat moored below us, "that you can live such intense and unforgettable adventures as the ones we are experiencing now. Just think— without our boat we could not be sitting here in this extraordinary place! Or, if we wanted to, tomorrow morning, we could set off, hoist the sails and head south, toward Suez, and be in the Red Sea to then proceed again to the Indian Ocean, moving beyond the horizon.

"What other means of transportation compares to a boat? What makes you feel as free, as autonomous and independent, allowing you to go in any direction you want without obliging you to follow a set course or road? And without needing to anxiously fill up a tank and pay for the fuel?"

"No other," she answered thinking it over, and added, "Truly."

ALIF

The large bay of Marmaris appeared before us in all its splendor. Our starboard had just flanked the lighthouse of Ince Burnu, which sat on the rocks, just a few feet from the sea, where a mocking wind blew.

We had left Bozuk Buku very early in the morning, after having said goodbye to Mustafà's wonderful family, promising them that this time we would return soon.

We'd had to motor on since there was no wind—a true pity, as normally the meltemi blows generously in the canal between the Greek island of Rhodes and the Turkish coast, assuring sailors exhilarating speed when they head toward Marmaris.

Nicoletta looked at me with an expression that by now I knew all too well. So I reassured her by saying, "Don't worry. I don't intend to suggest that we hoist the sails, now that we are almost there," and I added with a dash of disappointment, "but it is an ironic twist of fate!"

Marmaris Netzel Marina has a full range of services and is one of the best marina in the Mediterranean

Our destination was not the superb central Marmaris Netzel marina, nor the typical chaotic municipal tourist port, but a peaceful anchorage situated in the cove east of the bay.

We always opt for the privacy and remoteness of an anchorage rather than a busy marina. Naturally, this choice is only possible when no other vital practical needs prevail, such as refueling or repair.

The anchorage we were about to reach is beautiful not only because its natural context is simply marvelous, but also, if you need, for whatever reason, to reach land in your dinghy, it boasts a charming, peaceful, and very fine little hotel hidden among thriving palm trees. Its sandy beach ends on the dinghy dock of the Pupa Yachting Marina, located at the base of a short pontoon that rents out boats. It berths up to twenty charter boats, and some private boats, and offers freshwater and energy supply comparable to bigger marinas.

From the hotel, from 7:30 a.m. until 10:30 p.m., there is a *dolmus* bus that for a few cents, and in just a few minutes, takes you directly to the town center of Marmaris and back.

JANCRIS sailed the green waters of this huge bay, and keeping an eastbound course, we were enchanted by the brilliant green of the pine forest that covered the red soil of the hills, crowning the town of Marmaris and the bay. Nicoletta prepared to drop the anchor in the northern part, just behind the short promontory whose seafloor was muddy—an ideal spot for anchoring.

The small hotel, formerly an old residential house, with its arch-shaped beach and dock, had luckily remained unchanged. A few small box-like constructions, presumably bungalows, lay tucked in the shade of pine trees, strewn along the hill that sloped toward the bay's calm water. For years they have been the only evidence of an abandoned tourist project.

Nicoletta, as we went to stern to lower the white tender

into the water, happily commented, "It's still a very beautiful place."

"It's incredible that after five years, this place, just a stone's throw from the chaos of Marmaris, has not changed a bit, and nature here has luckily not given way to cement buildings, like the west coast of this bay." Pointing to a little paddle boat that was moving away from the dock I added, "Look, I bet those fishermen are going to lower their nets at the mouth of the river behind us, in the sandy banks, just like last time we were here."

Nicoletta looked up to see the small craft. Her slender, muscular arms, shiny from a tanning lotion, were flexed as she was holding the dinghy line suspended on the davit.

I helped her by releasing the opposite end from the davit's bollard so that the tender could be lowered gently onto the choppy water.

I mounted the Yamaha engine on the dinghy while the fishermen dropped their nets right where I thought they would. Then I returned onboard to absorb, for a little while longer, the gorgeous greens of the sea and forest around me.

Immersed in such peace, my mind travelled in time, taking me back to the summer of 1995—our first time here. We had followed the boat of some friends we had met at Gilles' shipyard, in Rhodes.

Their boat's name was ALIF, "the first letter of the Arab alphabet," Maruan explained when asked about the meaning of the word.

The son of a wealthy family from Cairo, Maruan had married a pretty young English woman named Debby, and together they liked to spend a few months every year at sea, onboard ALIF. The rest of the time they lived in London, Cairo and Hurgada, on the Red Sea.

With no financial restraints, they spent their life on their 36-footer. Budgeting carefully, they avoided waste and did all the general maintenance work on their own to keep ALIF perfectly efficient, as we, and most of our boating friends, normally do.

Not long ago, Maruan had discovered this anchorage haven by chance, and ever since then he was happy to come back to it, even if it was simply to fill up the water tanks or to take care of a little work while anchored.

One night, at dinner onboard JANCRIS, while we were anchored in a beautiful bay in Simi, Maruan convinced us to follow ALIF's course. They wanted to take us to a place whose beauty they greatly extolled and claimed to be ideal, but which on nautical charts did not seem well protected.

The decision to follow them proved to be a good one indeed. We spent about a dozen days in their pleasant company, our boats always anchored, while we travelled by bus into Marmaris to buy spare parts, or to have an artisan custom make them. The area known as "Sanai," which housed many industrial firms and artisan workshops, lay just outside the city limits.

One of the most memorable days there was when we paddled our dinghy upstream on a small river near our anchorage to catch sight of the freshwater turtles living along the riverbanks.

After roughly a few hundred feet, the vegetation radically changed from bamboo canes and other marsh plants to pine trees and colorful bougainvillea. A striking feature of the river was that there were no artificial banks to contain flooding, as in Italy. Instead, the reddish earth banks were clad in grass and plants that sheltered the turtles we had seen a number of times.

Unlike their tortoise cousins, these turtles swam fast. Their diameter ranged in size from four to ten inches, and their color was a dark gray-green.

Maruan advised us not to put our hands in the water since some of these turtles can be carnivorous; they may end up nibbling on whatever crosses their path.

Marmaris hosted a market each Friday, and close to this

area we came across a butcher shop that advertised wild boar meat available for tourists.

Happy to have made such a discovery, we walked into the shop and bought a leg. It was very cheap. That evening we ended up roasting the meat in the oven for dinner.

Once back on our boat, we were ready to say goodbye to the ALIF's crew.

The four of us were seated in the cockpit. The evening's highlight of conversation was our experience at the butcher shop. We recounted the story to Maruan—how we had run across the meat, and our surprise to see just how inexpensive it was.

"It's wild boar! Here, Muslims don't eat any type of pig meat so it's sold to tourists only," explained Debby.

"Right!" I interjected, "if it is only tourists who buy it, then it should be very expensive, especially in the summer when tourists invade the area."

"It doesn't work like that," she replied. "Wild boars abound here since they were never considered a source of food. The animal is only seen as a threat to the crops. As the human population abandoned the countryside, wild boars began to multiply rapidly, and the woods are now infested by these animals. It was only recently that the Turks began to consider the financial prospects that this animal can offer, but having business in their blood, sometime soon they will begin to export the meat throughout Europe— you'll see." And with a smile she added, "I am sure of it."

Incredible, how quickly these past eight years have fled, I thought to myself as I went downstairs to get a measuring tape, a pen, and paper, to measure a teak board which would eventually serve as a knife set. I was going to hang it in the galley. For a long time I had promised Nicoletta that I would make her a knife set for the boat, and this was the perfect place to have a carpenter cut it just right using professional equipment.

After taking the measurement, and writing the information down, I looked for the specific wood board I had set aside just a little earlier on.

"Fine," I said to Nicoletta who had been watching what I was up to for a while, "it is ready to be cut and become the knife set you have long been waiting for, which can be hung on the wall." Triumphantly I announced, "Tomorrow morning, as planned, we'll go to Marmaris, but before we head to the market, we'll drop by the carpenter I know in Sanai and I will get him to cut the teak pieces so they can be assembled when we get back onboard."

"It's about time," she replied, content, "I will finally have the knives handy instead of stacked precariously in hard-to-reach places. Boats require that each thing be in its place—just what our instructors in our sailing class always said."

The small buses called *"dolmus"* were very punctual and were easy to distinguish since the different colored stripes along their sides indicated their destination. In our case, we got on a bright pink *dolmus* that was impossible not to notice.

At nine that morning there was plenty of traffic, but there are never any real traffic jams there. We took our seats on the *dolmus*, the two seats just behind the bus driver. We had purchased our tickets, for a few cents, directly from the driver.

After about ten minutes we were already in the heart of the city. Though we had not set foot in Marmaris for years, many details resurfaced from memory, enabling us to reach the Sanai without getting lost or having to ask for directions.

Among the dozen little wood workshops and sawmills, we managed to find the carpenter we remembered. The individual workshops, all located within a single warehouse, stand close to one other.

Once inside, I immediately recognized the owner's face.

Like back then, his face was partly hidden by a bushy black mustache, which now had silvery streaks.

Naturally, he did not remember me. I showed him the work that needed to be done and thought he understood me. To be perfectly sure that the work was done as I specified, he asked me to follow him into the sawmill so that I would stop him if something was wrong.

It was simply amazing how he had stopped doing the work he was carrying out to dedicate his attention to me!

Using body language, we managed to understand each other, and within a few minutes the teak board was cut just as I had wanted it.

If that same work had been done onboard, and on my own, it would have taken me at least a few hours, and it never would have been as perfect as the cut made by machine.

When I was about to pay him, he told me—at least I think this is what he meant—that I could pay next time, since he had spent very little time on the task.

To be sure that there would be no misunderstanding, I handed him a bit of Turkish money, which he suddenly chucked to the ground.

I said goodbye and walked out of the workshop. Nicoletta, who had witnessed the entire episode, came up to me noticeably worried. She asked me if the man could have been offended by my giving him too little money.

"Don't worry," I said to her, "the first time I came across this custom, I, too, believed that the worker was offended by Maruan who seemed to have underpaid. Then Maruan explained that this is the local custom."

Moments later, I pointed out to her that the carpenter who had apparently refused the money, was now collecting the sum he had tossed away in the sawdust.

"You see, he did not want to be paid for petty work; it's part of their character and tradition. When I gave him the money and he tossed it to the ground, a little later, he picked it up—not like it was a payment for too petty a job that would not be worthy of him, but rather the way someone picks something up that he just happens to find on the ground."

The market in Marmaris is astonishingly big and bustling. Upon reaching it, we immediately mingled with the crowd.

The wide road right outside the center is closed to traffic during market hours. It is strewn with large canvas umbrellas, which protect not only the merchandise, but also the vendors and buyers from the merciless hot summer rays.

It has the feel of a bazaar since it features miscellaneous things ranging from Giorgio Armani jeans and Calvin Klein underwear to Ralph Lauren shirts and Dior glasses—all completely counterfeit, but well crafted.

The true highlight, however, and what brought us there, were the fruit stalls. They displayed their delicious fruit and vegetable produce in a strikingly artful way.

Pyramids were built of glossy, plump cherries, oranges so juicy that they seemed about to burst, crisp fresh heads of lettuce, arugula, a variety of tomatoes, onions, cabbage, yellow squash, zucchini. It's a truly picturesque and outstanding display of vegetables tasting as if they were home grown.

Also bound to catch the eye were the cheese stalls, especially the ones that sell goat and sheep-milk cheese. They also generally offer olives and homemade olive oil that is bottled in recycled plastic mineral water bottles.

Another popular set of products is honey and royal jelly. They are often sold from stalls that also sell a vast range of nuts, especially pistachios, and dried fruit in transparent nylon bags.

Spice vendors, too, have their unique attraction since they can be detected from afar, even before catching sight of them. The distinct perfume of curry fills the air around them.

Hot and weary, we went back home to JANCRIS with our knapsacks as full as sherpas'.

"I can no longer stand going into a city," said Nicoletta, placing her heavy bag on the saloon table.

"We not only rounded up a substantial amount of food but even had the pieces of wood cut, and now they are ready to be assembled. Then we can stay away from the world and we can do whatever we want," I then concluded, "and you'll see what a great custom-made knife can do to help your Geppetto craft you just what you want!"

GUIDE FROM MARMARIS TO BODRUM

Marmaris, Byzantine Cove, Serge Cove, Buzuk Buku, Bozburun, Keci Buku, Datça, Palamut, Knidos, Bodrum

Located southwest of the Turkish Asian peninsula, the Carian coast has a very idented littoral. The nautical charts show a long, narrow peninsula that protrudes westward and ends at Cape Krio (its Turkish name is Deveboynu Burun), with a lighthouse set atop. The peninsula south of Bodrum juts into the sea, creating two large, deep inlets. The desolate, arid land, sparsely covered with wild brush has forced its native inhabitants to look to the sea.

The area has two legendary ancient seaports—Alicarnassos and Knidos.

The Carian coast conceals the ruins of ancient Greek and Roman temples, old Byzantine churches and Venetian fortresses, hidden amid its vegetation.

Because of its barren land, this Turkish region has remained pristine, with no roads or cement buildings to mar the beauty of its landscape. It is a magical experience to drop anchor in a deserted bay, miles and miles away from noisy roads and smog.

In the most popular sailing anchorages small fishermen's restaurants can be found. These are simple but cozy places with tasty meals at affordable prices.

The two major sea towns in the area, Marmaris and Bodrum, are popular seaside tourist destinations. Visitors here find a vast selection of hotel accommodations and resorts that continues to expand each year.

The two towns are also ideal for wonderful sailing holidays since they offer luxury marinas, a large fleet of bareboat rentals, elegant charter yachts, and all the services a yachtsman may want. The wonderful climate, with warm summer temperatures

The ramparts of Marmaris Castle

from April to November, is particularly suitable for anyone wishing to enjoy a well-protected anchorage with the added value of having crystal clear waters for swimming.

The region of the Mediterranean Sea area that comprises Turkish and Greek waters has a characteristic regular summer wind called the meltemi. It blows north-northwesterly and is generally very strong during the daytime, diminishing at night, but sometimes the meltemi blows for days on end. Further into the gulf, the wind is lighter and allows you to sail in calm seawater.

If you are planning a visit to the Turkish coast in July or August, I suggest sailing from Bodrum to Marmaris since there is a good chance of sailing in comfortable and dry conditions during that time.

MARMARIS

The huge triangle-shaped bay, enclosed to the south by the small island of Keci and the Nimara peninsula, is set against a backdrop of green wooded hills, with the white buildings of the tourist town Marmaris perched above.

The approach to the anchorage and to the marinas, set easterly, is easy.

When visiting the town, be sure to see the ancient Venetian castle, in the heart of the old town and to take a walk at night in the Grand Bazaar that has hundreds of shops selling just about anything that you can imagine, and more. For dinner try the local specialties: the delicious and tasty "Doner Kebab" or "Chicken Kebab" and drink the local "Efes" beer. A good quality wine at a reasonable price is "Villa Do Luca" (9 U.S. dollars a bottle).

Marmaris Netsel Marina (36°51'.2N 28°16'.6E)

www.netselmarina.com

Netsel Marina is one of the most efficient and best-organized places in all the Mediterranean. It is built right next to the charming old town. It features: all-weather protection for 750 yachts up to 130 ft. L.O.A. in floating concrete pontoons, where yachts are tied stern to; each berth has access to a service box where you can get fresh water and electricity 240 V, 16 amps, both free of charge; toilets and hot water showers are clean and close to the pontoons; free wireless access; 24-hour security service; communication VHF Channel 6 laundry service, and car rental.

There is a yard in the marina and in addition to a 20-ton slip, there is a 120-ton travel lift. The area for dry storage isn't huge, and it is packed with yachts in wintertime.

This luxury marina has plenty of elegant boutiques and good restaurants, ship chandlery, supermarket and pool bar. A short walk to the old town offers a lot more shopping.

The price is 1.5 U.S. dollars per foot per day.

Marmaris Yacht Marina (36°49'.05N 28°18'.32E)

www.yachtmarin.com

This is one of the largest marinas and yards in the Mediterranean and it is rated "5 anchors" by the Yacht Harbor Association. The Marmaris Yacht Marina is two nautical miles by boat and six miles by car from the old town center of Marmaris. There is free transportation service, by small ferry, from Marmaris Harbor and from the Yacht Marina. There are 650 berths on the pontoon and many spaces on the hard standing. This is supported by three travel lifts for launching and storage of yachts up to 330 tons. A full range of services and facilities are offered for sailors and boats. There is a 24-hour security service on the property of the marina. Each berth has access to a service box where you can get fresh water and electricity 240 V. Toilets and hot water showers, free wireless access, laundry service, rental car, library, ATM and storage lockers. Communication on VHF Channel 72.

In the marina there are restaurants with international and Turkish cuisine, a supermarket, a chandlery, a fitness center and swimming pool.

The price for long-term storage and daily dock are very attractive.

Albatross Marina Marmaris
E-mail: albatrosmarina@superonline.com
This marina is about 1.5 miles from downtown. It is well protected from south, east, and west winds. The berthing capacity is 150 yachts, up to 130 ft. Electricity 240 V and fresh water in each berth.

It is possible to berth alongside or stern-to. Repair facilities, laundry, supermarket, fuel, bar, restaurant and other services are available in this marina and yard.

"Mavimar Yachting Professionals," based at Albatross Marina are responsible for the maintenance and repair of yachts in the marina and ashore. The capacity on land is for more than 200 yachts.

Entry Formalities
Marmaris, like Datça and Bodrum, is a port of entry in this region. Here the authorities provide the transit log, a cruising permit to sail on Turkish waters. The transit log can be purchased

in town for 30 U.S. dollars, and is valid for 365 days. All check-in formalities can be done personally or handled by an agent.

Transportation
Dalaman International Airport is sixty miles, a one-and-a-half hour drive, from Marmaris. The Greek island of Rhodes is 25 nautical miles south, and there is a ferry or hydrofoil connection daily that links the two cities.

BYZANTINE COVE (GERBEKSE IN TURKISH)
36°42'.1N 28°13'.6E
The ruins of an ancient Byzantine church, hidden among the silvery olive trees just a yard from the sea, probably give this tiny, pretty bay its name. Situated 15 miles from Marmaris, the deserted and peaceful Byzantine Cove can be either the first or the last anchorage on a trip to the coast of Caria.

Note the presence of a fisherman's restaurant at the end of the white cobblestone beach. Clients can moor free of charge on the buoys belonging to the small restaurant. A young man or the fisherman's son, on board a small wooden boat, help you to moor on the buoy, and will secure the stern mooring lines around the trunks of old olive trees. Don't forget that prices in Turkey must always be negotiated.

If all mooring buoys are taken the anchor can be dropped in 18.25 feet of water since the bottom is sand and grass, and therefore provides a good hold. The area is well protected from the meltemi and the turquoise water is very attractive for a refreshing swim.

SERGE COVE (36°35'N 28°03'E)
In all weather conditions, a safe anchorage is located 15 miles west of the Byzantine Cove. Without a GPS position, spotting the entrance of the bay is not an easy task because of a deceiving optical effect. As soon as the entry of the bay is visible, however, the approach and entry are simple and safe.

In fact, the cove takes its name from a pirate Serge who used it for many years as a hideout for his little fleet. This safe and spectacular cove is enclosed by rocky hills and to this day carries his name.

The Institute of Nautical Archaeology and Texas A&M University undertook an expedition to excavate the Serge Liman wreck during the summers of 1977-79. In 1978 the archaeological team directed by George F. Bass and Frederick H. Van Doorninck, Jr. discovered an eleventh-century shipwreck in this bay. It's possible to see some of the many types of glassware and ceramic from the ship's cargoes in the Bodrum archaeological museum.

The T-shaped cove offers two good anchorages. The little southeast bay is my favorite, with its turquoise water. Both are magnificent, and their wild beauty enchants the lucky people who drop anchor there. The sandy bottom provides a good hold, and also, in this case, you must fix a stern rope to the rocks ashore. The owner of the small local restaurant, Osman, is a fisherman. Located a few feet from the sea, his restaurant has a fine view of the bay. The best way to enjoy the cove is to walk up to the hill at the back of the restaurant, and relax as the sun sets, drinking an aromatic *Raki* on ice. If you intend to have dinner at Osman, try his fresh lobsters grilled.

BUZUK BUKU OR LORYMA (36°34'N 28°01'E)

This large natural harbor has been used since Greek and Roman times and is renowned for its picturesque landscape of wild scrubland. It is less than three miles west of Serge Cove.

Half a mile before the entrance of the bay, on top of the hill, there is a beautiful view of the old megalithic dry stone wall that protects the entrance of Loryma Bay.

Within the inlet, the water is calm and well protected. There are four good spots that are ideal for dropping anchor. A couple of small restaurants are located here and provide the possibility of mooring secured to a strong buoy.

My favorite place is in front of the small fisherman's tavern, a quarter of a mile past the entrance of the bay. Mustafà is the owner of the restaurant and of the mooring. Recently, if you decide to dine at his restaurant, he has set up a small wooden pontoon for docking that is free of charge. Every morning, Mustafà's wife cooks a tasty village bread in a big wood oven, and the air around is filled with the delicious smell of freshly baked bread.

Don't miss walking from the anchorage to the impeccably crafted old megalithic walls. It seems impossible that, centuries ago, people worked with such big stones so skilfully.

BOZBURUN (36°41.4N 28°02.6E)

After spending some nights gently rocked by the water in a deserted bay, it is always pleasant to stop in a small harbor. Docking here, you are close to a picturesque village, only 15 miles from Buzuk Buku.

The village of Bozburun is small but pleasantly arranged around an esplanade with olive and pine trees overlooking the port. There are several cafés and restaurants along the waterfront and a few small guesthouses near the dock, which occasionally allow yachtsmen to take showers.

After doubling Cape Karaburun, continue to sail north on the channel, between the rocky Greek island of Simi and the stretch of bare hills of the Turkish coast.

Even though the area you are sailing in is but a few miles from attractive Greek islands, I advise you not to stop in any Greek harbor or anchorage without having a cruising permit for Greece. Greek Coast Guards monitor the yachts in transit, especially those flying the Turkish flag.

The village of Bozburun, like the town of Simi, is an old center of natural sponge diving. Most shops along the main street sell unusually shaped natural sponges.

The village and its tiny harbor are located at the end of the large bay of Bozburun. The inner bay offers some good anchorages that are protected from the meltemi wind.

On JANCRIS, I used to drop the anchor between Kizil Island and the tiny island of Kiseli. If you plan to spend a night it is best to fix a stern mooring line ashore because irregular winds blowing from any direction are not uncommon. The crystal clear water makes diving from the boat impossible to resist.

Port Facilities
The reception dock offers space for more than forty yachts and has many extra berths for visitors. A small breakwater protects the port. Electricity and water are available. Diesel is available by tank truck.

The range of repair facilities is steadily improving and the number of skilled workers to date suffices to assure most major repairs.

Close to the harbor there are a couple of big boatyards specializing in woodworking, where the typical Turkish gullets are built.

Fresh fruits and vegetables, drinks, and other food supplies are available just a few yards from the boat.

Authorities
Customs office: Authorities from the local port charge for docking. Prices are less than a dollar, a foot, a day. The fees are collected daily, in the afternoon.

KECI BUKU OR ORHANIYE (36°36'N 28°07'.5E)
It is undoubtedly a good idea to sail for twenty miles or so in Hisaronu Korfezi if you have time, and also to spend a few days in the bay of Keci Boku.

The scenery of bare hills changes as you sail north and becomes a more verdant landscape. The barren regions turn into forests of pine trees, cedars, and colorful pink oleander, which line the calm emerald sea and at times make you feel as if you are sailing on a Canadian lake, since the surroundings are so green and full of tall pines.

All the restaurants, set on solid wood pontoons right by the calm seawater of this tranquil bay, offer hospitality, allowing to moor on their docks. The pontoons provide fresh water and electricity, a mooring buoy, and clean hot showers that are close to the pontoons.

All services are free for those who dine at the restaurants. In some restaurants, free docking is available if you buy just a glass of beer or Raki, the typical Turkish anise-flavored liqueur, which you can enjoy at a table just a couple of feet from the sea. The spontaneous and friendly welcome sailors get from the local people not only makes a very strong initial impact but also assures happy memories of this beautiful area.

"Iskele [Landing] Restaurant" is my favorite spot in the bay. My friend Izmed, the owner, years ago built a solid wood pontoon, and arranged very heavy mooring. There are berths for 15 yachts and all the facilities a cruising vessel needs. Just behind the dock there is a small restaurant where guests can eat by the sea. A candlelight dinner costs 25 dollars, berth included.

Do not miss a visit to the waterfalls of Turgut, less than ten miles from the anchorage. There is a thick forest of century-old trees, and walking in freezing cold water is a dreamlike experience in the summer, when outside of the forest the temperatures are as hot as an oven. The bravest can attempt a dive from the top of the waterfall and plunge into the tiny pool, twenty feet below. This excursion is a great break from sea life since it unveils the luxuriant vegetation that inland Turkey boasts.

Approaching the bay of Keci Buku by night can be dangerous. Pay attention to the sand bar that breaks the surface of the water here. This strip of sand stretches for two hundred yards, from the coast to the middle of the bay. In dim light, the rusty barrel that marks the end of the sand bar is very hard to see.

On the east side of the bay, the big marina and yard Marti Marina is very easy to see. This modern, full-service marina can berth more than two hundred yachts and has facilities that include a pool, a gas station, a pump-out, a restaurant and bar, a supermarket, an engine and hull repair service, a workshop, medical aid and much more. The price for a 50-foot yacht is 450 dollars per week. More info: www.martimarina.com

DATÇA (36°43'.4N 27°41'.3E)

In summer, if you are exiting Keci Buku bay and heading west, it is likely that you will have a headwind navigation. Even with the wind and sea against you, sailing to the harbor of Datça can still be fun since the wind is most often gentle. But if the meltemi wind blows hard, the crew and vessel must prepare for a wet navigation. When leaving the bay, it is best to leave early in the morning, before the meltemi "wakes up." In this area, the meltemi starts blowing at around 10 a.m.

Datça has preserved the look of an old fisherman's village, but don't be deceived by the tranquil atmosphere of this small harbor. Over the past few years, it has become a well-known tourist destination, and now many yachts are moored at the public wharf.

Ashore, just behind the boat, there are several nice, and expensive, fish restaurants. Late in the afternoon, each restaurant has display counters to show the catch of fish, mostly huge grouper, red dentex or silver swordfish, arranged on a bed of ice, and ready to be grilled. Many old stone houses that

Carpets for sale in Datça Harbor

Turkish vendors selling handicraft products or food to sailors

fringe the small harbor are now carpet shops. This typical multicolored, handmade Turkish product is exhibited in front of the shops, some carpets spread on the stone floor, others hanging from the display windows that open onto the beautiful harbor.

Don't miss the uphill walk to the center of the small town, where you can find many souvenir shops and the typical Turkish restaurants that sell tasty kebabs, *pide* and small grilled fish, at reasonable prices.

Close to the mooring, some antique shops sell interesting pieces.

Recently, many real estate agencies have opened offices here to sell properties and houses in the Datça area.

Port Facilities

Water and electricity are available along the entire pier.

Small tank trucks are available to refill yacht diesel tanks directly on the wharf. If you need diesel, ask the harbor agent who comes around in the afternoons to collect the port fees from the yachts moored at the wharf. For a 50-foot yacht, in 2008, we paid 50 dollars per day. Electricity is not included, and there is an extra charge that depends upon consumption.

There are some good supermarkets that provide plenty of choices and are ideal for stocking up on your food supplies. All supermarkets deliver your purchases free of charge to the boat but it is always is best to ask beforehand.

Authorities
Datça is a port of entry. Port authorities that attend to all the customs clearances, in or out of Turkish waters, are walking distance from the harbor.

PALAMUT (36°40'.17N 27°30'.19E)
Set in a beautiful green valley against a backdrop of bare, gray rocky hills that reach inland, Palamut is a tiny village where time seems to have stood still through the ages.

The long, plain Baba Island shelters a small portion of the Datça Yarimadasi desert coast, allowing the formation of lovely white beaches that glitter under the intense summer sun.

Two of these beautiful beaches line the tiny tourist harbor. Recently the inner part was dredged so that there is a depth of 10 feet of water everywhere. When you approach the entrance, the stone and concrete breakwater finally appears, but from afar it is difficult to locate. Scattered houses hidden by the foliage become visible once you reach the calm harbor waters.

It's pleasant to walk along the one village road that ends near the harbor. There you'll find some restaurants, a few shops, and a couple of small grocery stores. That's all there is. Late in the afternoon, some restaurateurs who own seafront property prepare tables on the beach. Dinner by candlelight will undoubtedly be an unforgettable and romantic experience. The air is filled with the music of tumbling stones washed rhythmically back and forth by the sea.

The inlet's water is pristine and transparent—from the boat, you can see the anchor chain many feet below. The beach bordering the tourist harbor is bathed in clear, irresistible seawater.

Port Facilities
Transit yachts can drop their anchors and moor on the east or west side of the harbor, securing a mooring rope on one of the bollards on the jetty.

Electricity and fresh water are available ashore. However, it isn't easy to refill the diesel tank.

The mooring fees are reasonable, and a 50 ft. yacht costs in Datça costs 50 dollars per day, including electricity end water.

Usually the man who helps with mooring maneuvers also collects the harbor fee.

Ashore
Fresh bread and little grocery stores can be found close to the harbor. A couple of grocery stores are located a yard from the mooring.

KNIDOS (36°41'.3N 27°21'.8E)
The ancient ruins of the temples of Knidos, founded by the Spartans, stand here and there along the surrounding slopes and seem to tower over the well-protected bay, lending the anchorage a mysterious beauty. It is a moving experience to see the solitude of the hills now and to imagine how big and busy this city must have been two thousand years ago.

The old city was famous for three reasons: its gigantic marble statue of Aphrodite, portrayed in the nude (now you can only see the foundations and three steps of the podium of the round temple), a scientist named Eudoxus, and a renowned medical school.

When approaching this memorable anchorage, pay attention to the northeast breakwater. It is ten feet below the transparent water, so it is best to navigate in the center of the channel. The bay offers good shelter from the meltemi wind, even when it is blowing hard.

The anchor can be dropped in fifteen to thirty feet of water; the bottom is a mix of sand and seaweed. One section of the anchorage is totally covered with *Posidonia* seagrass, so your anchor can drag. The best option is to drop the anchor at the very end of the bay where the bottom is mostly sandy.

To visit the archaeological site you have to buy a ticket at the small ticket office close to the beach. It is an incredible experience to walk around there, and to sit in the old Greek theater in front of the bay where your vessel is anchored.

Even if you are not keen on archaeology sites, Knidos is an anchorage that must be seen.

BODRUM (37°02.1N 27°25'.5E)

Once you have passed the stately Cape Deveboynu Buru and its magnificent lighthouse, about 25 miles to the north, you will find the large touristy city of Bodrum.

If the meltemi wind blows, the sail from Knidos to Bodrum can be a demanding one. It will be uncomfortable and wet. For this reason I suggest setting off early in the morning.

Approaching the harbor of Bodrum during the day is easy, while in the dark it is hard to find among all the city lights.

The renowned Castle of St. Peter overlooks the harbor's entrance from the east. Once in the calm inner water of the harbor, if you look westward, you can see the gas station and the Bodrum marina's floating pontoon. Eastward are the customs office and the daily trip berth for the Greek island of Kos.

Private or charter yachts, inside the harbor, can be moored only in the marina pontoons and not along the public wharf. The public wharf is for the local vessels and gullets.

Like the Marmaris marina, the marina in Bodrum boasts efficient services satisfying the needs of cruisers, and is located at walking distance from the city center and from the shopping area.

Don't miss seeing the Castle of St. Peter and its interesting archaeological museum, one of the richest and most important in the area.

The ruins of the Mausoleum of Alicarnassos unfortunately do not reflect the magnificence of the big and important city.

Close to the marina you can see many seafood restaurants, all quite good, though not all have good prices. I suggest reading the menu closely before sitting down.

Port Facilities
All-weather protection for 450 yachts. Electricity and water in each berth. Security service 24 hours, seven days. A dinghy that helps to dock the yachts. Clean bathroom facility with a large number of hot showers.

Laundry and dry cleaning.
Supermarket with free delivery of purchases to your vessel.
Gas station in the entrance harbor.
Possibility to repair most everything, painting, carpentry, electrics, electronics, engine (Volvo, Yanmar, Perkins, MTU)
70-ton lift. E-mail: teknoege@superonline.com
Ship's chandlery
Wi-Fi connection
Consultant for international entrance and exit procedures at the marina office.
Milas (Bodrum) International Airport is only 20 minutes from the town center.
www.miltabordummarina.com

Authorities
Bodrum is a port of entry. Customs authorities, where all clearance formalities can be dealt with, are available near the harbor.

GENERAL INFORMATION
Undoubtedly this area presents some difficult sailing conditions when the meltemi wind blows strongly. It can be downright dangerous near Cape Deveboynu Buru. But the many well-protected anchorages in the region help make the sailing less difficult.

For crews that have little sailing experience, I suggest renting a yacht with a skipper so you can enjoy a great holiday and improve your sailing techniques.

All the charter companies have a list of good skippers—ask when making reservations.

Weather

The good season is from April to November.

During July and August, the meltemi wind normally blows force 6 or 7, sometimes even more in wind acceleration zones, creating rough seas, especially near the promontory and the channels between the islands. Northwesterly and west-north-westerly winds predominate.

In the remaining summer months, in spring, and in autumn, the winds, though coming from variable directions, are lighter. Northwesterly winds prevail.

Rainy days are very rare throughout the summer season.

Reference Pilot Books

We have sailed the area using *Turkish and Cyprus Waters* by Rod Heikell.

Navigation Rules

There are no forbidden navigation areas along this coast.

Yachts flying the US or EU flag undergo easy and simple entry procedures.

The "Transit Log" or cruising permit for Turkish waters expires after one year and costs 30 U.S. dollars. A foreign yacht that spends the winter in a marina or yacht slipway, and is used by the owner at least once every two years, may stay in Turkey for up five years without having to obtain further permission.

The passport visa expires after 90 days and costs 20 U.S. dollars.

Connections

Many airlines that fly to Dalaman and Bodrum are low cost and charter flights. The Dalaman airport is sixty miles from the center of Marmaris, and in 2008, the taxi cost 100 dollars. The Bodrum airport is only 30 minutes drive from the center of Bodrum.

Daily trips from the port of Bodrum can be made to visit the Greek island of Kos by small ferry or hydrofoil.

From Marmaris, the Greek island of Rhodes can be visited daily by small ferry or hydrofoil.

Distances

Marmaris – Byzantine Cove:	18 miles
Byzantine Cove – Serge Cove:	15 miles
Serge Cove – Bozuk Boku:	3 miles
Bozuk Buku – Bozburun:	20 miles
Bozburun – Kecy Buku:	20 miles
Kecy Buku – Datça:	25 miles
Datca – Palamut Harbor:	15 miles
Palamut Harbor – Knidos:	10 miles
Knidos – Bodrum Marina:	22 miles

Useful Addresses

Ankara United States Embassy, 110 Ataturk Blvd.
Kavaklidere, 06100 Ankara – Turkey
Phone (90-312) 455-5555 fax: (90-312) 467-0019
e-mail: webmaster_ankara@state.gov

U.S. Mission: Istanbul, Adana, Consulate Agent in Izmir

Ankara British Embassy, Sehit Ersan Caddesi 46/A, Cankaya
06680 Ankara – Turkey
Phone +90 312 455 3344 fax: +90 312 455 3334

British Consulate-General in Istanbul, Mesrutiyet Caddesi
n. 34, Tepebasi Beyoglu 34435 Istanbul
Phone +90 212 334 6400 fax: +90 212 334 6401

Australian Embassy in Turkey, MNG Building Ugur Mumcu
88, Graziosmanpasa 06700 Ankara
Phone (90-312) 459 9500 fax: (90-312) 446 4827
e-mail ankapassports@dfat.gov.au

Australian Mission: Istanbul, Canakkale

Canadian Embassy in Ankara, Cinnah Caddesi n. 58, 06690
Cankaya Ankara, Turkey
Phone +90 (312) 409 27 00
e-mail ankra@dfait-maeci.qc.ca

Some useful Websites
Marmaris International Yacht Club: www.miyc.org
www.sailturkey.com, www.bodrum-museum.com,
www.datcarehber.com, www.turkuaz-guide.net/
bozburun.htm, www.datcainfo.com
www.allaboutturkey.com/likya.htm

PART 2

The Lycian Coast: From Marmaris to Fethiye

The Lycian Tombs

With the sun still high above, JANCRIS' teak deck was warm.
I was reclining comfortably on a soft, waterproof foam rubber cushion upholstered with Sunbrella canvas and was enjoying the scenery and some good music. I had no other
agenda in mind, at least for the time being.

Our navigation of roughly twenty miles, the distance
that separates Marmaris from the verdant bay of Ekincik,
seemed incredibly short thanks to the intense meltemi wind.

We moored, as we had done in the past, in the eastern
part of the bay. Here, an ambitious restaurateur had built a
functional dock amid the rocks. After having first lowered
the anchor, we moored to stern and secured the lines on
rusty iron rings that were planted right in the rocks.

We were immediately struck by the large number of

vessels—the quantity had notably increased since we were last here. Fortunately, though, the surrounding landscape remained practically unchanged, with its green woodland of pine trees whose dark branches extended waterward.

There was no sign of cement or paved roads—only the restaurant, which for years has been standing here, hidden amid the plants some thirty feet behind the pontoon.

How great it was to be able to do nothing and not have to conserve time; or to worry about chasing the clock hands as they tick, always late for things.

When it all started, and we changed lifestyle, I could not conceive that days could be spent so calmly, without being constantly engaged in something "constructive" that only complicated life. Indeed, back then, I had simply transferred my city lifestyle onto the sailboat since I believed that the passing of time only meant something if time was used to its fullest, making the most of every single second; otherwise I would get bored to tears and feel useless.

I still recall how intoxicated I had been by urban city life: working all day on my plans. How could I have known that a different lifestyle from the one I was familiar with existed?

Needless to say, I am now sure that I was wrong, but back then, spending time comfortably, outlandishly, soaking up the sun and looking around inquisitively, to observe the world, was simply inconceivable.

But after getting to know Turkey, it often happened that I would find myself with my nose in the air for minutes at a time, enthralled and grateful to have witnessed the flight of birds that designed complicated arabesques in the sky to then disappear into the green woodland.

Or on long journeys across the oceans, I contemplated the seawater, so motionless and at the same time mutable. I still like to watch the surface of the sea, which captivates and hypnotizes me like the crackling of flames dancing toward the sky.

Many years were needed for me to change my ways, to live onboard and to perceive the new universe around me.

Gradually, month after month, my own rhythm began to harmonize with the rhythm of Mother Nature, as I became ever more attuned to the boating life.

Now, I no longer feel guilty when I spend my time doing apparently nothing.

To lay down relaxed, fully conscious of what I am doing—that is nothing—is to me an enormously gratifying sensation. Taking some time to myself, and currently I have been doing this more and more often, I admit, to think and ponder things over, would certainly be impossible if I were busy doing something else.

To live in direct contact with nature encourages you to learn and spend time observing her, as this is the only way to get to know to her.

City life does not require such acute observation, and contact with nature is less direct. Nature and the world are outside our windows or behind a wall, with no direct inter-action: you don't need to feel the wind on your skin, as it is not important, to see what direction it comes from, or if it changes direction, if it gets colder or it fades away. It does not matter, and it does not affect daily life.

When, instead, you live on a boat, or in the mountains, failing to pick up on the changes in the direction of the wind may be fatal. For this reason, it is essential to see what is around, to observe the sky, sniff the air, and sit doing nothing except listening to the universe whisper to you.

In animals, and this includes man, any change, and nature's mutability, must be observed to prevent disaster. Such conduct assures survival.

I smile at the thought of how much my companion Nicoletta and I have changed in the past ten years we have lived onboard. From the very start, she enthusiastically supported my desire to radically change our lifestyle, and together we are now happy to live the only life we have, our way. Over the years, we have molded it to suit our needs like a pair of new shoes, which, after being used a little, become comfortable and fit you perfectly; similarly, our life has granted us the satisfaction of becoming perfect for us.

The smile on my face turned into one of curiosity when my reverie was interrupted by a man's voice, uttering English words, from the pontoon.

"Mister!"

I turned toward the man who was calling me. "Mister, do you want to make a trip to Caunos tomorrow morning?"

"What does he want?" asked Nicoletta moving to stern.

"He wants to know if we would be interested in visiting the archaeological site of Caunos," I replied.

"We already saw it a few years ago, but I would be happy to go back to see the rock tombs, perhaps avoiding the site of Caunos," she proposed.

"All right," I said, "let's see how much it costs so we can negotiate the price," and descended the gangway to reach the burly young man who was waiting, with a red cardboard folder in his hand, probably containing the leaflets describing the trip.

After a short conversation and some bargaining, the price of the boat trip was determined—thirty dollars per person—and this included taking us along the Koycegiz river in the morning and coming back early in the afternoon.

"Seems like a wonderful trip," said Nicoletta happily as she crossed the gangway to get back onboard. She added, "I'll take advantage of a swim to check whether everything is okay with the anchor and chain. Since we'll be gone half the day, I want to be a hundred percent sure that it doesn't drag." With these words, she grabbed her goggles, went to the bow, and dove into the clean aquamarine water of the bay.

As I retrieved my mask and mouthpiece to join her, I saw her stop where the anchor lay, raise her arm out of the water, and with her thumb pointing up, signal that the anchorage was perfect.

In the morning, as we agreed, the young man with the olive complexion and a short, sparse mustache pulled his long light-blue boat up against ours.

We gracefully jumped onto the boat and pushed his boat away from JANCRIS to avoid a possible collision.

The single cylinder engine picked up revs and sputtered away from the bay heading toward the mouth of the river, which was about three miles long.

That day there were no other clients onboard and we could sit on any of the bench seats covered in multicolored carpets.

The helmsman, at the stern, was sitting cross-legged smoking a cigarette, and, shaking his packet in front of us, he kindly offered us one.

The day was sunny and clear; the sea, flowing swiftly beneath us, was a cobalt blue. The closer we drew to the mouth of the river, the greener the water became.

The beautiful strip of white sand that protects the estuary like a breakwater was lined with multicolored beach umbrellas and bathers.

Once we passed the entry to the strait, the green water became still and blended with the reeds of the marshes on the horizon.

As agreed, we avoided stopping at the ancient site of Caunos to see its ruins and followed the winding river that, like a silvery snake, uncoiled to reveal a vast labyrinth of cane fields.

Our experienced helmsman proceeded upstream without the slightest hesitation, even along the secondary waterways.

When we rounded a bend, he slowed down and pointed to a rocky wall on a hillside that was not very far away.

There, masterfully sculpted in the reddish rocks, appeared, as if by magic, the marvelous façades of Lycian tombs that for millennia have bewitched the travellers lucky enough to see them.

While our eyes delighted in such beauty, I took quite a

few pictures which, over the years, I have used to illustrate the articles I write in the Italian monthly yacht magazine called *Vela e Motore* [Sail and Power]. Nicoletta went to the bow to see the extraordinary works of art from up close. Then, unexpectedly, as in a mirage, the cane fields suddenly disappeared and gave way to a broader and sharper vision of the landscape.

On our way to the village of Dalyan, a parade of rock tombs unfolded to our left. There, we got off the boat and walked along the village roads, to see the town's small, crowded bazaar.

In the distance, you could spot the craggy rock that housed the Lycian tombs. The imposing Lycian rock tombs with their facades curved into the form of temples were the last resting place of the kings of Caunos. We thought it worthwhile to stop once again to contemplate the scenery. Meanwhile, lunch consisted of a tasty mutton kebab, which was very spicy. After our meal, we returned to the blue boat that was waiting for us at the small wooden pontoon.

Lycian rock tombs seen from the Dailan River. Their facades are curved into the form of temples

We got aboard and headed toward a thermal spring. Our helmsman claimed that, "when a sore or sick part of the body is covered with hot mud, it does miracles since it heals it forever."

When we reached our destination we got off and noticed that tens of boats, just like ours, were moored there waiting for their guests to return.

The thermal area features a big house with a black iron entrance gate.

Inside, the garden has a few tables and white plastic chairs where guests can have a beer or some other drink while waiting for their turn to go into the thermal water and cover their bodies with its dark mud.

Curious about the whole thing, we approached the scene but found such an overwhelming crowd of people all covered in mud, from head to toe, that we thought it best to return back to our craft.

No further words were needed. We looked at each other, turned on our heels and left.

"We are lucky not to be in pain or sick. Otherwise, I would have felt guilty to have left as we did," said Nicoletta once she was back on the boat, releasing the mooring lines to return onboard JANCRIS.

"I think that very few people were there for health reasons. Most of the people there are like us, European tourists who are simply curious," I replied, feeling content with our choice to go back home.

Ancient Lydae

The 1800-square-foot gennaker was hoisted with ease thanks to the great sock that our friend Umberto, a sail maker at UK-Halsey had designed for us.

Nicoletta had wanted this incredibly useful sail, with a three-point electric-blue star in the center, to be a lemony yellow, "to be seen from a distance," she had told Umberto last winter, when we went to Verona to ask his advice.

We wanted his opinion regarding our upcoming long voyage away from the Mediterranean on the Atlantic Ocean—whether he thought it best to be equipped with a light genoa or a smaller but heavier gennaker.

He had no doubts: for our long-haul journey, and since our crew was only the two of us, he preferred the gennaker instead of the two old spinnakers that were still onboard from our previous circumnavigation.

But, on ocean crossings with light trade winds, he advised us to use the spinnaker during the day, and the gennaker at night when maneuvering is more demanding and dangerous. He assured us that he would be happy to custom make our heavy gennaker, one that would be easily manageable—as small as possible without compromising the typical gennaker design—yet would withstand the hardships of twenty-five-knot wind gusts without tearing.

Painstaking attention went into the sock: a fundamental part that had to be artfully designed down to the finest detail, using only the most technologically advanced and resistant material that is lightweight but doesn't trap air.

A well-made sock can be brought down and stuffed in its case like a sausage in any weather condition, quickly and without difficulties.

In fact, since we have had our new gennaker, the two old spinnakers, a medium sized one of about two thousand square feet, and a lighter one of about two thousand four hundred square feet, with which we travelled the world, have not been mounted at all.

A weak following wind filled our large yellow sail, which reflected its color onto the blue water, conferring to it a strange and surreal yellowish hue.

Running with the wind, and with a calm sea, our speed was good and cruising was comfortable.

The more than twenty miles that had separated us from

Cape Kurdoglu were already behind us, so we could take down our gennaker, and close it with the sock.

Right in front of the cape, as if by magic, the wind suddenly dropped and disappeared. We had to proceed by engine to the large bay of Fethiye.

Seeing how late it was, we decided to moor in the first place mentioned in the cruising guide, one that had the unpronounceable name of Kizilkuyruk.

Nicoletta had spotted, from a distance, the prominent red rocks that mark the bay's entrance. Once inside, we saw a pair of well-protected anchorage points in a beautiful cove at the end of the bay that tapered like a funnel, ending on a pebble and white sand beach.

JANCRIS, with the engine on low, headed slowly into the bay where a few boats were anchored, their mooring lines secured to the rocks on land, or around the trunks of big pine trees near the shore.

It was the first time we had visited this anchorage with its wild beauty—the green of pine trees a striking contrast with the brick red of the steep rocky cliffs, which are bathed in the blue sea north of the bay.

The anchorage located north of the little inlet had been taken by an enormous gullet whose hull reminded us of a pirate ship.

We therefore turned westward, to where the bay ended and became a completely empty little white beach.

"Terrific! This is just the place!" I thought as I directed the prow toward the beach.

Close to shore, the gently rising seafloor became completely visible through the transparent water, enabling Nicoletta to pick the best spot to drop the anchor.

On the deserted beach, a little inland and positioned exactly in the center, stood a large bushy olive tree that was the perfect place to secure our stern line.

JANCRIS, in no time, was berthed in pole position. Its stern, a few feet from the narrow beach, was set against a backdrop of steep hills, and its bow pointed toward the exit of the bay.

"What a marvelous place!" said Nicoletta enthusiastically. "This beach is practically all ours and it is so well sheltered that it's almost as if JANCRIS is docked in a port."

"It is truly spectacular—we are totally surrounded by pine trees and olive groves; no city noise, and best of all, no dumping of deadly toxins into the sea," I said cheerfully as I walked to stern to dive into the inviting, crystal clear water.

The need to check how well an anchor is dropped presents a perfect excuse to go swimming, and it should become a habit anyway, as it will tell you whether the anchorage is safe or not.

After eating a plateful of pasta, we lay on the cushions at stern wrapped in darkness, quiet and half asleep, or rather, totally relaxed.

The piercing chirp of crickets saturated the air and the melancholic call of a solitary owl echoed from the tall invisible hills, which had been swallowed by the darkness of the moonless night.

On the water, the reflection of a few amber lights that emerged from the portholes of the moored boats were a reminder that we were not the only vessel anchored there.

The hot dry air from land, laden with an intense perfume of resin and sage, lulled us into complete surrender to Morpheus' embrace.

Nicoletta woke up in the middle the night and had me follow her to our cabin. The air was totally still, and the portholes of other boats were now pitch dark. Only those skippers who go by the book keep their anchor lights on, which, as they are set high, blend with the glitter of stars. For a second I stopped to watch the stars in awe. They had never seemed closer—perhaps I was still dreaming.

In the morning, a rattling of iron roused me from bed to take a look around. That sound is all too familiar to me now, as it signals that a boat near us is getting ready to set sail. As I poked my head out of the companion, I watched the chain come up quickly thanks to the anchor winch. After they cleared their anchor, as they were heading out of the bay, I realized that their roughly forty-foot boat had been chartered.

When they had arrived, I had checked, during one of my swims, to make sure their anchor was not crossing our chain.

Yet in a bay as tight as this one you never know what can happen. It is therefore good practice to always double-check things.

With the sun already shining and hot, I looked at the big brass clock sitting next to the barometer of the same shape, that hangs over the bulkhead of the navigation table.

Since it was eight o'clock, if we wanted some shade and protection from the heat, which would otherwise prove un-bearable, we would have to mount the canvas at stern. Only then could we dive into the water for a refreshing treat, I thought, standing there in my bathing trunks.

The very warm day passed lazily, between swims and maintenance work. We usually think that we'll spend an hour, at most, but instead, on more than one occasion, half of our day has been spent this way.

Our trips away from the seawater were planned for late afternoon, when the temperature once again becomes bearable.

"I read that ancient Byzantine and Roman ruins can be found by walking inland, in the hills. How about it? Are you up to seeing the ancient, abandoned city of Lydae?" I asked Nicoletta whom I could see approved my idea, as she was already nodding with a smile.

The tender took us to the beach and, with our socks and running shoes, we hiked northward, and followed a clearly marked, winding path that led to the top of the steep lofty cliffs that overlooked the bay.

Once we lost sight of the sea, the stone-paved path widened in some places. And the hike, in some sections, became less strenuous and demanding. Along the way, the pinewood offered its shade and was an idyllic spot to catch our breath.

After an hour of walking in the middle of nowhere, we unexpectedly encountered two well-built dark gray stone houses.

We approached them and figured out that they were probably the remains of small cathedrals that had incorporated previously existing temples, erected centuries earlier.

All around us lay hand-carved stones and fallen columns with richly adorned capitals. We sat on top of one of the remains to contemplate the view all around.

From where we sat at the top of the hill, stretched a splendid panorama of verdant pastures on which cattle grazed.

Further away, the gentle hills covered in pine trees declined seaward toward the inlet of Skopea, which from here was hidden from view.

It proved an evocative and mystical spot—and a special pleasure since it was utterly unexpected.

"Who can tell how many more surprises this Turkish coast will have in store for us," said Nicoletta looking around, adding, "I think this land is unique. It is too vast, and fortunately too untamed to be spoiled by mankind in the third millennium."

WING SOUTH

At the end of September, back in 1996, while we were on the Greek island of Crete in the port of Heraklion, we met, for the first time, a young Italian man named Ito.

His boat, WING SOUTH, was moored next to ours. When abroad it is only natural to spontaneously approach someone who comes from your own country and befriend him.

During one of our conversations he confessed that he felt

a little down, as his girlfriend, a few days before we arrived, had had to go back to Italy, to start working.

Sailors also never to miss an opportunity to arrange a meal with friends, even if they are brand new friends, and so we invited him onboard JANCRIS one night for dinner.

He was a very pleasant and charming guy who entertained us with exciting boating stories, especially his adventures sailing among the beautiful islands of Venezuela.

The night before our departure, he surprised us not only with an invitation for dinner on his cozy American-built boat, but also with his outstanding cooking ability.

"I had a restaurant for a few years," he revealed, in his deep, husky voice, by way of justifying the excellence of his dishes.

We were sorry to leave him behind, alone, but we had to move on from the enchanting island of Crete and sail toward Rhodes, since by mid-October, JANCRIS had to be taken out of the water for the winter season.

In any case, after many years away from home, he too would soon go back to Italy and spend the winter in the town of Biella, with his parents.

But as we had promised him in Crete, we managed to stay in touch from time to time that winter. We even discovered that he had taken our advice and had decided to "park" his vessel in Rhodes as well.

In early March, on a hot, sunny day that anticipated the arrival of spring, we finally left the city of Padua to return to Rhodes, the island of the Sun God, aboard our boat. Our summer plans were to sail along the Turkish coast—from Fethyie to Antalya. All our friends knew our itinerary and we, in turn, knew their courses and destinations for that summer of 1997.

Exchanging individual navigation plans has always been a great way to know where your boating friends are, and to see if the routes cross so that you can take a little detour and spend a fun evening together sharing experiences.

And now, thanks to the Internet and to e-mails, or even simply SMS, it is even easier to keep in touch. Back in those globetrotting days, you could only rely on SSB radio.

All of our sailor friends who had actually been to the inlet of Skopea and Fethiye had words of praise to depict its beauty, but never did we imagine that we would see such a sublime place and moor in such a spectacular protected bay, where the hours and days just flew.

The charming fishermen's village of Göcek truly bewitched us, and even Gemiler and Tersane, with their alluring beauty, were extremely hard to leave behind. Proof of this comes from the fact that in July we were still moored in the bay of Fethiye, putting us two weeks behind schedule.

Of all the bays we had visited, Fethiye was so spectacular and ideal for boats that we had lost all awareness of time. Besides, when it comes to sailing, plans are made to be changed!

We reached the anchorage facing the town of Fethiye late Thursday morning. It was a technical pit stop since we had to replenish our food supplies with fresh fruit and vegetables, and its market, held on Fridays just outside the city center, was perfect. Because we did not need water or fuel, we dropped the anchor near a group of five or six yachts, just opposite a shipyard located west of the bay, and thus avoided docking at the municipal wharf where dozens of caïques were berthed.

When I lowered the dinghy onto the water, I noted with disappointment that the sea color was green and not particularly inviting to swim in.

All around, instead, plants thrived, such as the tall upright pine trees that like church steeples, or should I say minarets, soared toward the sky.

Several little hotels, camouflaged amid trees, were strung along the surrounding mountainsides. Like sentinels, they seemed to herald the town, which is dominated by the uniformly white box-like constructions that run along the sea front. A little further east, rock tombs magically appeared on the vertical, red rock mountains.

Lured by them, I took the binoculars, which I keep on-board, to observe them. A few of the tombs were remarkable for their large size and for their delicate, elegant ornamentation.

"Nicoletta, do you feel like walking to visit the tombs that we saw as we approached the bay?" I asked her. "They seem wonderful."

"Why not?" she replied enthusiastically, adding, "Give me a few minutes to get changed, and we can go."

Indeed, just a few minutes later, our white Arimar dinghy sped over the calm sea. With its deep fibreglass keel, its 11-foot size, and the reliable 15 hp engine, this craft is more than just a simple means of transportation to and from land. Indeed, it is a true dinghy, always stable and dry. When a lot of your time is spent aboard, and you are avoiding marinas and ports as much as possible, a good dinghy is indispensable as a means to reach land regardless of weather conditions—possibly even with dry feet.

On the municipal dock, we found a quiet corner where we tied the bow of the dinghy.

At that time of day, the paved waterfront promenade, with its white and red tiles, was not crowded, but there were vendors selling pistachios and ice cream. Sitting lazily behind their stalls, they waited for the sun to set beyond the horizon, to alleviate the torrid heat that only daring tourists defied.

From the waterfront, we detoured onto side roads lined by all sorts of shops selling just about everything. Because of the hour, the sellers standing outside trying to lure passers-by into the shops were not in the best of shape. This enabled us to head straight to the market area just behind a nearby square. The low-rise building that houses the market has handicraft shops all around its perimeter, and areas dedicated to the fish market and the vegetable market.

Walking swiftly, we passed a seemingly endless row of ironmonger and fabric shops until, all of a sudden, we found ourselves in front of a large open area, a sort of entryway that led to the real market.

It was virtually impossible to resist the temptation of seeing the market, so we proceeded onward to the inner square from which the pungent smell of fish and goat cheese arose and mingled with the shouts of vendors and the hum of the crowd all around.

At the center of the little square stood an imposing circular counter, richly decorated with vibrant marble tiles, covered in ice and displaying all kinds of fresh fish and shellfish.

Inside this enormous ring, vendors screech at top of their lungs to tempt the last customers of the day to buy their fish before closing time.

Along the fishmarket perimeter, butcher shops line the market area. They sell their meat whole or in parts, with half a cow ready for carving, or smaller skinned animals ready for roasting, all hanging from huge steel hooks.

Cheese shops are mixed in with the butcher shops. They showcase different shapes and types of cheese, fresh or aged, and rich creamy yogurt sold in big white plastic containers, all kept behind a glass door, in a refrigerated counter. Opposite the fishmarket square, the other gate led us to the fruit and vegetable market with many richly fragrant spice shops.

This was yet another bustling area. The fresh, multicolored merchandise was masterfully arranged on the stalls, and above, on the wood beams, hung long braids of gray garlic arranged next to purplish braids of red onions.

Garlands of emerald green and fiery red chili peppers announced their spiciness with their bright hues. The duller brown garlands next to them, which were funnel-shaped, attracted my attention. Hesitantly, I approached them and sniffed the suspicious objects from up close to discover that they were made of wild mushrooms that came from the nearby woods.

After crossing through this colorful market, we found ourselves in front of another gate, but this one opened onto a road, and into the blazing, blinding sun.

The road surface, and its uphill grade, only intensified the effect of the heat, as we followed the brown road signs pointing the way to the tombs.

Luckily, my army green wide-brimmed hat, which I had bought in Australia, protected my head, and my airy Reef sandals allowed me to walk comfortably.

Nicoletta, with her long tanned legs, kept her pace up even if now and again, the heat irritated her and made her huff and puff.

At a certain point, she grumbled, "It's incredible how, with all the time we have, we end up torturing ourselves this way. We could have left JANCRIS at a more suitable time, later in the afternoon, to climb all the way up here."

"You are right," I replied, "but since we don't know how late the tombs are open, I thought it was best not to risk . . ."

She did not reply, but her fatigue and frustration due to the heat vanished immediately, as we suddenly came upon an ancient stone sarcophagus with an impressive pedestal and lid, right in the middle of the road.

Surprised, we moved closer and touched the ancient artifact with our hands to make sure that it was not a mirage, but a real stone sarcophagus dug from the rocks, who knows how many millennia ago.

"Look where this sarcophagus sits," said Nicoletta, amazed, "in the middle of a road with cars and trucks driving next to it. Isn't it incredible?" she asked, looking at me, as if expecting a response I could not formulate.

I walked around the sarcophagus a couple of times and saw that it had a hole on one side of the roof-shaped lid. The hole on its side was a little less than one and a half feet wide. Someone must have made the hole to see what was inside, who knows how many centuries ago.

"Let's go," I said, taking her hand and proceeding upwards.

A notice on the front gate announced that the site was open to visitors until 8 p.m.

I shifted my gaze from the notice to Nicoletta's face. She in turn stared back at me with an expression that fused amusement and anger.

"Don't say anything," I warned her, and continued, "to be forgiven, I will buy your ticket to visit the tombs," I proposed, a little embarrassed.

A steep dirt road ascended to the rock tombs. The beautiful, elegant façade of Aminta's tomb had been dug out of the mountain rock back in the 4th century B.C. Its exquisitely sculpted Ionian columns, its ornaments and headpiece evoked the same awe as a Greek temple.

And as I turned to catch Nicoletta's eye, I was struck by the sheer magnificence of the view just behind me.

The tomb seemed to hover over a breathtaking panorama. The view encompassed the whole bay of Fethiye, extending to the mountains northward, and stretching to blend with the milky light blue of the distant horizon.

Below my feet appeared the red rooftops of city homes and the minarets reaching gracefully toward the sky.

Further down, the water in the bay was as still as a lake, and like a blue mirror, it reflected the woods that surrounded it.

The white hulls of yachts were riding, at low speed, the calm seawater; other boats there drowsily dozed, anchored in the middle of the bay.

How beautiful, I thought, and looking away my eyes searched Nicoletta's. She was standing between the columns, in front of the tomb. Like me, she was enchanted by the overwhelming beauty of this spectacular bay.

"The inhabitants of this land certainly knew how to

JANCRIS sailing under the meltemi wind

choose the most mystical places. So much beauty is over-whelming—I can't tell whether it is this amazing landscape, or the finely crafted tomb façade just behind me that strikes me most," and with an agile jump that brought her down from the tomb she added, "Maybe both, since for thousands of years they have been inextricably entwined and one complements the other. The inlet of Fethiye would not be so charming and interesting without the tombs, and the tombs would not as fascinating if they weren't in such a breathtaking setting."

I nodded in agreement, and we slowly headed back to the dinghy.

The afternoon thermal wind blew in rather violent gusts from the direction of the sun, which by now was beginning to set.

The tender, tied to a cleat of JANCRIS' stern, bobbed fitfully right and left, like a fish trying to free itself from a hook.

Nicoletta, seated at the pilot table, was preparing the shopping list for the following day, while I was working away trying to fix the flashlight, which seemed determined not to work any longer.

Out of the blue, a knock on the hull and a voice from outside calling "JANCRIS, JANCRIS!" startled us both.

At once, we got out, and to our utter surprise, we immediately recognized Ito. Standing on our dinghy, he was holding on to JANCRIS' side, to our stanchion, to prevent the wind and current from carrying him off.

With a smile on his tanned face, he extended his arm, ready to shake my hand.

His boat, WING SOUTH, was anchored some sixty feet from JANCRIS. With its sails furled in a disorderly fashion, and sheets not properly cleared, we could see that he had wasted no time in mooring before coming to see us.

We invited him onboard and the moment he set foot on deck, he hugged us and sat down in the cockpit. There, thanks to the rigid cover that assured us shelter from the wind, we could sit and tell each other all about our recent adventures.

Time passed quickly, and dinnertime found the three of us sitting once again around JANCRIS' cozy dinette table, exchanging funny anecdotes.

On that occasion, Nicoletta announced that next year we would leave to circumnavigate the world, and she was therefore curious to know about his Atlantic crossing experience.

The joy suddenly drained from his face, and his expression hardened as he said: "I can only tell you about my one crossing, and I don't think I will repeat the experience again," and stopped there.

Upon hearing these words, Nicoletta turned to me with a withering look.

There goes all my psychological work, I thought, down the drain; my trying to convince her, for months, to promise me that she would accompany me on a novel adventure; in a few seconds, and thanks to Ito's words, it all suddenly seemed in vain. But moments later, when he had reorganized his thoughts, he went on to say, "It was really hard, since there were only two of us. Me and my travel mate, a Venezuelan, who had no previous offshore experience. We left Venezuela and sailed the Caribbean Sea following its natural arc which island after island leads northward. Until then, navigation had been very pleasant. We had seen wonderful places, and I must admit that the islands of Los Roques, in Venezuela, are no less beautiful than many of the most sought-after destinations; quite the contrary.

"From Puerto Rico we decided to undertake a longer navigation to the islands of the Bahamas. When we had set off, the weather conditions were initially favorable but the further north we sailed, the more the conditions degenerated with each passing hour. We ended up regretting having gone to sea since we had another five hundred miles to go.

"Luckily, and despite the rough sailing, when we reached the Bahamas, our boat was intact, though we were dead tired since our shifts at the wheel had been so demanding and strenuous. The stopover in the Bahamas helped us to recover our strength and get WING SOUTH ready for its upcoming long journey.

"Day after day, the little group of sailboats that intended to launch themselves on the long-haul sail across to Europe grew and became more consistent.

"The long days of stopover, while waiting for the weather conditions to improve, were really fun. At least four times a day, we would meet for a beer at the yachting club bar to exchange the latest updates and share our knowledge with others who were waiting for the same thing.

"There were the 'Captains Courageous', as we nicknamed them, who in words, and as long as they were on land, feared nothing and would even tease the overly cautious, blaming their 'crybaby' wives for not allowing them to undertake the journey.

"One day, tired of waiting and encouraged by the great

forecast, I raised the anchor and sailed eastward, in the direction of the Azores. Another five or six sailboats sailed on our slipstream, and with our newly acquired friends, we kept in touch via radio twice a day to find out the position of each boat and to chat and keep each other posted.

"As for the fate of our 'Captains Courageous' and their crafts, our group saw no trace of them. They had stayed put, their anchors dropped in the Bahamas. As our boats paraded past them, our prows toward the coral reef pass, they saluted us from the dock.

"During the first days of our journey, our navigation proceeded smoothly, with a good average speed, covering a sizable distance per day. Then, you can guess, the wind turned and had us sail close-hauled all the way to the Azores, making the journey seem endless and very uncomfortable.

"Those long days were like living in a washing machine: with gigantic waves rocking us, and splashing into our cockpit. Many nights were rainy. Temperatures got colder and colder as we approached our destination, and bathing ourselves was out of the question in those conditions. But day after day, our bodies adjusted, until one morning when, as if by magic, we seemed capable of achieving acrobatic miracles—like heating soup on the gas burners.

"After eating some warm soup, absorbing its heat, and allowing it to permeate our whole bodies, we felt much better and even our humor changed. Our vital energy, that some time ago had seemed drained, was recharged."

"So you went from America to Europe..." I interrupted, without waiting for a reply, and went on, "All the sailors who have crossed the Atlantic in both directions say that the voyage eastward is much more difficult than sailing westward. What do you think?" I asked, hoping his answer would support the points I had made, and would convince Nicoletta to undertake the around-the-world tour, or at least try the experience of an Atlantic crossing, as a first step.

"Navigating the Canary Islands and the Caribbean is undoubtedly simpler. Moreover, the weather conditions in this southern part of the world are more predictable and stable, not to mention its pleasantly warm temperatures," he concluded.

While he was talking, I had watched Nicoletta's face gradually relax, and in the end, smile at me as in a sign of solidarity.

I had done it!

We would participate in the Millennium Odyssey and circumnavigate the world together, at least up the Caribbean. The thought delighted me. To celebrate the exciting project, I filled the glasses with a good red wine Ito had brought for dinner, and made a toast to the journey, our dreams, and the Atlantic Ocean.

The following autumn, we sailed from the island of Gran Canaria to Saint Lucia.

The Atlantic Ocean crossing, our first ocean crossing, proved to be a wonderful and memorable experience for both of us. In fact, Nicoletta ended up accompanying me all around the world, and she did not miss even a single mile of the more than 25,000 miles of navigation.

An outstanding crew member, Nicoletta participated in everything, from being at the wheel to working on the sails without any hesitation, even in the worst winds or with huge waves that made JANCRIS's prow shoot up and then quickly fall without a moment's rest.

For the record, the Atlantic crossing leg of the Millennium Odyssey 1998-2000 Cup ended rather well for us: we came in fourth overall, and were the winners of our category. At the end of the circumnavigation, we placed third overall.

Ito, three years after our dinner onboard JANCRIS, crossed the Atlantic Ocean once again, this time on a friend's 44-foot aluminium sailboat.

On this particular journey, he went westward, landing on the Brazilian coast, and then sailing south, almost to the end of the South American continent, to the Tierra del Fuego, in Ushuaia, the last outpost before Cape Horn.

In the meantime, WING SOUTH was peacefully berthed in the warm sun of the island of Rhodes, looked after by our friend Gilles in his shipyard, waiting for its indefatigable owner to go back to sea in pursuit of another of his dreams.

Tersane

"Do you remember," I asked Nicoletta as we passed near the small island of Tersane, in the rugged gulf of Skopea, "the year 1997, when we moored on this island after having spent a happy week anchored in Fethiye, together with Ito?"

"How could I forget such a wonderful place?" she answered, her eyes set on the Mediterranean vegetation that carpets the gentle hills of the tiny island we were approaching. She went on, "Let's hope it hasn't changed, and that the anchorage is as charming and peaceful as it was. I'll never forget the way we spent our nights lying on deck, sheltered by the rocks that encircled the little bay, gazing up at the star spangled sky, so bright it almost seemed within reach.

"The only light that shone on land was a green light placed on a palm tree just a few feet from shore. The green cast gave it a surreal appearance, like a fluorescent figure emerging from pitch darkness to swallow everything around it. The sea was incredibly still. Its surface, like a mirror, reflected the overarching sky, its dome of stars giving off a silvery light like sparkling white Christmas lights."

As we neared the narrow entrance of the bay, Nicoletta went to the bow and unfastened the anchor from its place.

At stern, a neatly coiled 200-foot floating line was ready for use.

In such a small bay, it is important to fix the boat's stern and secure it to a rock so that even if the wind changes direction the boat does not move.

We passed through the short entrance canal, and suddenly the panorama of the entire bay unfolded before us.

Because it was early morning, the bay was semi-deserted and our former anchorage spot was free. Hence, without a moment's hesitation, I veered north, orienting the bow toward a rock by the seafront, about 150 feet from us. Nicoletta dropped the anchor releasing plenty of chain, which clanked its way into the water.

In gear, I throttled and directed the boat toward the rock for approximately another thirty feet, and then quickly veered 180 degrees with the stern now facing the rock.

At my signal, Nicoletta grabbed the floating line and jumped into the water. In a jiffy, her blonde hair resurfaced from the water, and I saw her swim swiftly to the rock and tie the rope around it.

When this was done, I got into reverse gear and brought the boat closer. Nicoletta was watching my maneuver from her perch on the rock, some fifteen feet away.

From stern, I retrieved several feet of rope, which had to be made taut, and then fastened to a bitt at stern.

I then moved to the bow and pulled up the excess chain to secure the boat.

A few minutes were all that was needed to anchor.

As I turned the engine off, I raised my eyes to look at Nicoletta ashore, and noticed that, still wet, her body glistened in the sun rays, which beamed down on her sculpted muscles and her long slim legs, making her look like a bronze statue atop a rock. The thought that this beautiful woman was my wife delighted me.

Just then, she slowly slipped back into the water, and I dove in to catch up to her.

The clean, though not transparent, water refreshingly embraced me; it was my first swim that day, and certainly not the last in view of the heat.

A little later, we got back onboard and went to the bow to dry our bodies and soak up some sun. But since the sun would soon become too hot to bear, we decided it was best to mount the very large canvas cover to ensure plenty of shade.

We were about to finish tying the canvas straps in place when we heard the distinctive roar of an excursion boat's engine—one of the boats that carry an unbelievable number of tourists all packed on board, daily.

With its blasting music, the engine fuming black smoke, and the racket of its passengers, it was quite a spectacle. We watched, dumbfounded, for a few minutes, and were greatly worried by the anchorage maneuvers of the boat's captain.

A stout young man suddenly dropped the large anchor, and in a matter of seconds, it was dangling dangerously from the bowsprit.

The engine was turned off, and a tattooed chubby blonde woman, wearing a barely visible bikini, announced to clients, with the help of a loudspeaker, that the "diving and swimming party" was now starting.

The announcement triggered a movement onboard. Suddenly most of the passengers dutifully headed to stern to descend the ladder; the more daring dove from deck instead, showing off their diving skills in very amusing performances.

The boat was moored smack in the middle of the little bay, just over the presumed position of our anchor. Annoyed by this, I watched people invade the water all around the boat and disperse, like an oil slick.

Just then, another similar boat, approaching at great speed, also headed our way. It too was packed, and, as I had guessed it would, it lowered its anchor next to the other vessel—fortunately, and miraculously, managing to avoid running over those swimming close to the boat.

On its slipstream, a third boat pulled into the small bay, filling it completely.

The latter was another overcrowded sixty-five-footer with loud music playing full blast. Half an hour is what it took to radically disrupt the peace and quiet of the bay. Such clamor caused a couple of private sailboats, which had been anchored there even prior to our arrival, to leave and seek a quieter haven.

Nicoletta turned to me, as I was sitting under the shade of the canvas, still observing with incredulity what had happened some thirty feet away, and asked me what I intended to do next.

"We'll wait and see what these people are up to," I answered, and after a brief pause said, "Judging by the precarious and dangerous way they anchored, I doubt they will stop here for long."

And indeed, no more than a few minutes later, a horn sounded. Its echo bounced off the deserted hills; simultaneously the engine released a black cloud of fumes, engulfing in smoke those bathers who were coming up close to the rest of the crowd and trying to make their way up the ladder to get back onboard.

Over the loudspeaker, the young woman's call urged the few bathers who had swum to shore to get back onboard. Her nasal voice could probably be heard all the way to Göcek, five miles away.

Seeing that the first boat had began its maneuvers, the other two crafts followed suit and also began calling their guests, to make sure that all those who had dipped into the water just a few minutes earlier, would be aboard.

Almost touching when maneuvering, the long wooden boats moved out of the bay in the same order they had arrived, and then they all sped away toward another destination.

Almost miraculously, and in a very short span of time,

the anchorage again became the enchanting paradise I so fondly remembered.

Once again, crickets, with their non-stop singing, filled the bay with their music, interrupted only by the odd "hee-haw" interlude of donkeys that were hidden in the shade of the ancient olive trees.

For years, the nearby olive trees had not been cultivated. They grow next to reddish rocks that are carpeted by vegetation and covered in a consistent layer of dust because it almost never rains.

East of the bay, where the depth of the water is less than three feet, there is an impassable inlet.

Centuries ago, before becoming sanded-in, the inlet was surely the entry to an ancient shipyard, as evidenced by the remains of old stone buildings and other ruins of smaller buildings lying further inland.

Near the shore, having always been a feature of this site, sits a little Byzantine church. Further inland, some buildings have been partially restored and made habitable by the only family living here. The family also runs the small seafront restaurant on the southern tip of the bay, which we remembered being lined by a few tall palm trees.

Some of the other ruins were fenced off to keep the goats and chickens away.

Nicoletta joined me at stern, under the canvas and away from the sun, where I was sitting comfortably, like a pasha, on cushions.

I moved to make some room for her.

"What peace," she sighed, and turning to look all around added, "For a moment I feared we would have to spend the day in the unpleasant company of those boats and their blasting music. They must be the excursion boats that offer 'eight bays in half a day' trips to tourists, including lunch." But she soon turned more cheerful as she said, "Anyway, it's much better to have a half hour of noise and traffic, knowing it will soon disappear, than to have hotels with their guests permanently spoiling a bay. Fortunately, all of Skopea is practically intact. Its landscape has not been changed over the years by new buildings or roads, though a few more boats have appeared. But, after all, we must consider that this is peak tourist season, and a beautiful area like this deserves to be seen by many people, for half an hour or more; the important thing is not to cover the coast with buildings—when an excursion boat has no customers, it stays in port, but hotels, even when empty, stay on."

"On the other hand," I interjected, "we cannot be so selfish as to think that we are the only ones who have a right to enjoy these splendid spots. We mustn't become solitary sea-dogs, like some of the people we know, who just can't stand being around others, conceiving life on a boat as being away from everyone and everything, that is, leading the life of a recluse."

"You're talking about Paolo, right?" she said, unable to hold back her laughter.

"Right, and he's not the only one." Smiling myself, I affirmed, "An increasing number of acquaintances of ours, who live on their boats, want to escape the society they were raised in. I don't criticize this, but the idea of avoiding all people, even the inhabitants of the places that host them, seems too much."

Having said that, I got up, moved to stern, and dove into the refreshing water of the bay. When my head broke the surface, I tried to imitate the nasal voice of the tattooed woman on the tourist boat, inviting Nicoletta to join me because "the diving and swimming party" had just begun!

She jumped in and immediately reappeared a few inches away from me, saying, "I like staying in touch with society and meeting people," and after taking a deep breath, added, "What I don't want is to revert to the mores of a society that were imposed on me before we changed our lifestyle. We now realize that you can live differently, both with a greater inner peace, but also more harmoniously with others. This newly found inner equilibrium is not only very satisfying, but it has also enriched us, since less materialism has made us more romantic, and allows us to appreciate the simple things in life. It's all about following our dreams and our hearts rather than preset targets and profit," she concluded smiling.

And I . . . could not resist kissing her.

Gemiler

Just after we doubled Cape Ilbis, leaving the magnificent inlet of Fethiye behind, our sails, which until a few seconds ago were well rounded by the puffing wind, were now without the slightest breeze, limp, and wave after wave, our mast and tacking vibrated.

I turned the engine on so JANCRIS would once again be back on course. Without the rocking of the waves, we were able to douse the sail and neatly furl it.

The island of Gemiler, our destination, from a distance seems to be joined to the mainland, but since we were quite familiar with the place, this optical illusion did not fool us.

We knew that in the narrow channel that separates Gemiler from the mainland coast, we would encounter a well-protected anchorage that shelters vessels from the meltemi and large waves.

As you move closer, the ruins of an ancient Byzantine city can be seen sitting amid the many olive trees that cover the little island.

Roughly six hundred feet from the mainland, the channel that separates Gemiler comes into view. When it had fully unfolded before us, I veered to starboard and started looking for a place to drop the anchor.

Moving along the channel, a small motorboat pulled up close to JANCRIS. One of the two young boys aboard asked Nicoletta, who was already at the bow ready to maneuver

the anchor, if they could help us tie our stern line on land—
like in almost all bays in Turkey.

Nicoletta agreed, smiled, and thanked them.

Their boat then slowed a little more, ran along our slipstream, and they waited for us to decide where we would
haul our anchor.

Once the spot was identified, Nicoletta released the
windlass, plunging the anchor and chain into the deep blue
water, while I engaged the reverse gear and moved back.

The two boys on the red fiberglass boat, with a large
white line running all around it, moved to within a few
inches of our stern. Nicoletta then handed them the long
floating line we always use to secure our boat to land.

The boy at the helm speedily moved to shore and his
friend jumped off to knot the line to a rock that sat some
feet behind us.

As nimbly as they'd jumped on land, they bounced
aboard again and came back toward us.

I thanked them, fully conscious that they were expecting

Gemiler Island, with a Byzantine church on top of the hill

Going for a swim. Paradise Bay, Gemiler

something from us. Indeed, one of the two, who seemed very alert, told me that he was the son of the owner of the taverna. It was not far from where we were, on the beach, opposite the island of Gemiler.

He added that the house specialty was great grilled fish and tasty meat kebabs.

Smiling, I said that we thought we would eat on JANCRIS but that we would be happy to have an ice-cream in the afternoon, when they would have a chance to be there, and that the following morning we would be happy to have some "village bread," the typical wood-baked bread you find along the coast, which stays fragrant and is delicious for several days.

The boy's face gleamed with a satisfied look. He nodded in agreement and said they would be back in the afternoon. I thought to myself that their day did not go so badly after all. And just then I saw them rush off toward another sailboat that was about to enter the channel.

I joined Nicoletta who was sitting at the stern contemplating the spectacular scenery offered by Gemiler.

Its steep slopes were scattered with evident signs of ancient dwellings man had left behind, centuries ago, now invaded by Mediterranean vegetation.

Some buildings are just rubble, mounds of stones; others, instead, still have well-preserved stone walls; others still, very few in fact, were spared by violent events over the centuries and you can still guess their layout, including part of the roof.

No matter where we turned, there were ancient human traces everywhere.

Just over the rock where our boat was tied, I spotted a round oven still intact; a little further on, I spied small patches of colored plaster that had withstood time and still clung to the stones that were once the inner walls of a house.

Even beneath us, a few feet under the surface, there were the remains of a citadel that had been swallowed up by the sea owing to the phenomenon of bradyseism [slow fall of the earthcrust], which to this day afflicts this area.

JANCRIS was floating over the perimeter of a building, which thanks to the transparency of the water, we could admire as easily as if it were above water.

"Let's snorkel and see what's down below," proposed Nicoletta, who was dying to swim amid the ancient ruins.

Once we were in the water, the impression I'd had of its exceptional transparency was confirmed. You could clearly see more than sixty feet below, an extraordinary sensation— like flying above the seafloor.

JANCRIS' hull cast a dark shadow beneath, offering shelter to small fish hiding from bigger predators.

Silvery and sinuous troops of mullets swam in apparent safety, and further below, the diffident blacktail lived hidden in the rocks that were formerly a home to humans, now lying several feet below our boat's clean blue keel.

In order to make the most of the unique beauty of this

place, in the afternoon we decided to go for a walk around the historic site.

A pleasant and talkative young Turkish man ran the site, and entertained even the laziest tourists with richly detailed accounts of what they were missing if they kept sitting on the beach instead of getting around to see the place.

His true intent, of course, was to sell his cheap entry tickets and homemade guides in English and German that provided information on the ruins found on the island.

Picturesque views unfolded from the steep bumpy path that leads to the uppermost part of the island, as it winds among the partly destroyed cluster of houses and small Byzantine churches.

Nicoletta was carrying a small knapsack with a camera inside, as well as a couple of Efes beers and some potato chips, which were quite necessary, as we needed to enjoy a quick refreshment on the bare hilltop at sunset.

I carried a digital camera on my shoulder so that I could capture the beauty of the setting sun there to show my friends at home.

On a large hilltop that lay a little below our destination, we came across the primary attraction of the entire site, the cathedral, which was adorned with rich marble and colorful mosaics.

Walking by, we noticed that some young people, who had Oriental facial features, were working near the imposing altar.

Nicoletta said, "They are part of a Japanese archaeological expedition. They have a permit from the Turkish authorities to do research work and excavate around the entire island," adding, "While you were tying the dinghy to the rock, and I was waiting for you to join me, I overheard the man selling tickets explaining that to an elderly English couple. They were white as milk and did not feel like hiking all the way up here."

I felt a breeze of fresh air across my face, my welcome

to the summit, where there was an unparalleled view, 360 degrees.

Nicoletta looked around to see where it would be nicest to have a snack, comfortably seated, as the sun was about to set the sea ablaze.

The sea below us was smooth and looked almost like a thick skin, striped here and there by tiny waves produced by the current, which made bright purplish ripples on the surface, as if that enormous expanse were alive.

Eastward, the woodland covering the hills hid the beautiful lagoon of Olu Deniz and its soft white sandy beach, where, in spring, sea turtles of the Caretta Caretta species lay their eggs, and where now, instead, the beach umbrellas of vacationers dominated.

Nicoletta and I have tried to capture and immortalize on film the peace and sublime beauty of the location at the best time of the day: when the sun-soaked earth is slowly wrapped in darkness. During this period of transition, and thanks to the fiery light, which produces elongated shadows, the edges of the jagged rocks appear smooth.

We sat on the ground, still warm from the sun. We sipped our beers, taking in the slow but inexorable changes that happen in a matter of a few minutes every day after sunset: The turquoise sky above amazes us, as its delicate clouds, threaded through with many shades of vermilion, drifts slowly over us, heading south.

GUIDE FROM MARMARIS TO FETHIYE

Ekincik, Kyzil Koyruk Koyu, Skopea Bay, Göcek, Cleopatra's Bay, Tomb Bay, Tersane Island, Boynuz Buku, Karacaoren, Gemiler Island, Fethiye

This Turkish coastline carries the same name as the people who have lived on this land since the 2nd millennium B.C.—the Lycians.

The rocky and wooded coast is in some parts very dry, due to the powerful Mediterranean sun, while in other areas, it is covered in luxuriant pine forest. It is always picturesque and filled with history.

Famous worldwide are the Lycian rock tombs, which are carved from the rocks and sit embedded in the mountains. They were made by the Lycians as a fitting final resting place for their loved ones.

One of the many anchorages in the Bay of Fethyie

In the ancient days, the imposing Taurus mountain range protected the inhabitants of the coast from invaders; now the Taurus protects the natural beauty of the coast's splendid bays from the unregulated building of new tourist villages.

Imagine yourself in a deserted bay that is sheltered on all sides from the wind, immersed in luxuriant Mediterranean vegetation and carpeted with pine trees or dotted with ancient olive trees. And imagine clean seawater whose tones range from turquoise, to gold, to orange over the course of each day.

All this is reality when you sail along the coast from Göcek to Fethiye.

And many more unforgettable experiences are guaranteed—like great swimming, great sailing, exciting trips to archaeological sites—and this is no travel agency pitch, this is truly what you get when visiting the Eastern Mediterranean sea.

Sailing is a great way to see the area and explore it. Boats can be chartered one way from any of the modern marinas of Marmaris or the marina of Göcek or Fethiye.

If you already own a boat and intend to cruise in the Mediterranean Sea, be sure not to miss this unique area.

It is no problem to change crew there, as the airport is not far from the marinas. The well-organized marinas offer an excellent place to meet up with friends and family to start a great Turkish cruise.

MARMARIS
See Part 1, page 38

EKINCIK (36°49'.4N 28°33'E KARACHAY LIGHTHOUSE POSITION)
Outside the busy Gulf of Marmaris, you'll need to turn your prow eastward along the coast. The wooded bay of Karaagac is prohibited to pleasure boats because the area is a military zone.

Sailing on, you encounter the bay of Kocegiz. Pay attention in the area because there, submerged just a few feet below the surface of the cobalt sea, lie a dangerous group of rocks.

Opposite the lighthouse of Karachay, which indicates the entry to the cove of Ekincik, there is a long, private wooden jetty, which is the most sheltered position in the whole bay. The sea here is ten to fifteen feet deep and has a sandy bottom, providing a good hold when you drop anchor. Secure two ropes on the jetty, but make sure not to get too close to shore as there are some big rocks that jut out from the bottom and can therefore damage the rudder. In this case you need a long (ten feet) and safe gangway.

The transparent, attractive, warm water of this anchorage will no doubt make you feel like going for a long swim. Be sure not to forget to check your anchor position and the rudder situation abaft with your diving mask.

Usually ashore, two young men on a dinghy are available to help sailors moor in the jetty. The pontoon is for yachts in transit that intend to stop and dine at the restaurant on the hill. From the deck, you can spot the restaurant hidden among the pine branches. The pontoon is also a safe place to leave the boat to enjoy a half day trip to the ruins of Caunos or to the renowned Lycian tombs along the Dalian river.

Mooring is free of charge if you dine at the restaurant. Note that in the late afternoon, one of the young men on the dinghy, with the pretext of collecting garbage from the boats, asks whether you are going to eat at the restaurant. If the answer is "yes," the boy calls the restaurant, via VHF, and books a table using the boat's name. If not, the trash disposal will cost you a hefty tip, as it must be discarded far from the dock.

Hot showers and the toilet facilities are located on the ground level of the restaurant, and are, of course, free of charge.

To refill your water tanks there is a long rubber hose connected to the restaurant, but make sure to ask the dock worker for permission before proceeding.

Freshwater is usually free, but last summer, the man assisting on dock asked to be paid since a considerable quantity of water was consumed by the owner of a yacht moored next to JANCRIS.

The restaurant is perched on the hill that overlooks the jetty and it boasts not only a breathtaking position looking out over the bay, but also five-star service.

Compared to standard local prices the menu is expensive, but it cannot be regarded as costly since the service and quality of the cuisine are high, and in the end, the bill is similar or cheaper than what you would pay in a good restaurant in the U.S. or Europe.

As an alternative to the place I've just described, there is an anchorage at the end of Ekincik cove, near the small village, in front of the sandy beach. Here you can have more privacy, but with strong meltemi winds, the anchorage can be rolling, if not dangerous. Ashore, some restaurants offer grilled fish or meat for a reasonable price.

Another anchorage is found to the west, just before the lighthouse of Karachay. The bay, with its pine forest, has some well-protected little coves where anchorage is possible before a wild backdrop that is sheltered from the prevalent summer wind. Though huge caiques are found anchored here, the smallest coves are perfect for normal cruising vessels. Unfortunately the deep water, about sixty-five feet deep, and the seagrass bottom, confer a dark green tone to the clean sea water. Note also that since seagrass covers the bottom, it is best to test whether the anchor is firmly fixed before tying your mooring line around a big trunk ashore. In this bay it is important to fix a line ashore because with the hills that enclose the anchorage, late in the afternoon and at sunset, a strong wind blows from different directions. At night the wind disappears and the bay is filled with the music of chirping crickets.

In all these anchorages, local wooden tourist boats selling tours to Caunos and the Lycian tombs up to the Dalian river will approach your vessel and a friendly, smiling man will illustrate the half-day trip he offers to see this wonderful area.

My advice to you is to go and see this unique and unforgettable spot. The only way to navigate along the Dalian River is by embarking on one of the local tour boats—and don't forget to bargain the price down. Then, at last, all you will have to do is to relax and enjoy the natural beauty and the great Greek and Roman ruins. This trip alone is worth the entire vacation.

SKOPEA LIMANI (36°34'.1N 28°49'.5E) LIGHTHOUSE ON PEKSIMET ISLAND

In summertime, the conditions of wind and the sea are favorable for sailing south and southeast-bound. The thirty miles from Ekincik to the bay of Fethiye can usually be covered quickly. The west side of this huge bay hides another big and well-protected bay called Skopea Limani.

Mother Nature seems to have created this area with yachts in mind. In this magical expanse of sea, vessels can drop their anchors in wonderful, safe bays and sail in calm cobalt water past tiny deserted islands and green creeks, where time appears to have stopped centuries ago. It is one of the most striking areas of the Turkish coast.

Red rocky cliffs tower over the deep blue Mediterranean; other cliffs, eroded by the sea, have become dark caves. Pine and oleander grow on the gentle slopes of the surrounding hills and are mirrored on the calm, transparent water.

The boat is the only way to reach this area, and for that reason, the experience proves unforgettable. Here you can sail for weeks, changing anchorage every day and enjoy cruising, taking advantage of the thermal wind that blows gently in the afternoon. Even though the bays are only a few miles from one another, each bay is distinct and different. Each stone here lies as a witness of ancient events and of a culture which was lost in time. And on the sea, or at walking distance from the vessel, you can still see today the ruins of the history of this unique land.

Some of my favorite anchorage spots are located here, and the mooring possibilities this bay offers number in the hundreds, all well protected from the sea and the wind in summertime.

When leaving Ekincik, sailing to the bay of Fethiye, the first anchorage that I suggest is on the northeast side of the big bay, in a cove called Kizil Kuyruk Koyu.

KIZIL KUYRUK KOYU (36°37'.2N 28°52'.2E)

This peaceful anchorage is a good place to relax after the fairly long navigation from Ekincik, or before leaving the area to sail up to Göcek. Inside the bay you will find two coves, ending in a small stony beach.

When dropping the anchor, you'll find that the bottom is sandy and rocky, and not an excellent holder for it, though the depth for anchorage is adequate even close to shore. As usual here, you can fix a line securing the stern to a smooth gray rock.

Well protected from the meltemi wind, the anchorage is set in a gorgeous natural context. The steep hills all around are covered in pine and olive trees, and the sea is as transparent as glass.

A path, which is easily found, leads to the ancient ruins. It crosses a beautiful pine forest and climbs uphill to reach the site. Be sure not to miss this easy walk in the hills to catch a glimpse of the ruins that for centuries have slept in this magical spot.

GÖCEK (36°45.1N 28°55.3E)

For many years, the fishing village of Göcek has been famous among yachtsmen, and for this reason its economy revolves around yachting services. This charming village has escaped mass tourism and the waterfront is a pleasant walk where no cars are allowed.

Göcek is the best place to start a sailing journey in this area, for it boasts several modern marinas offering full service and it is only a twenty-minute drive from Dalaman International Airport.

Though in the last few years new luxury marinas have been built close to the village, the old municipal marina remains the best option, for its position is right in the heart of the village. Camper & Nicholsons mega yachts berths are located on the southwesterly side of the bay.

If you are spending a few days in Göcek, I suggest trying the municipal dock first. It is usually very busy, but also very conveniently located. If you want leave your boat for a longer period, it is best to contact a safe marina and to visit it beforehand.

There is also the option of dropping anchor in the bay and going ashore with the dinghy. JANCRIS is usually anchored in front at the short beach near the village in twenty feet of water. The ground there makes a good holding place.

Nicoletta and I tend to prefer the privacy of an anchorage, since on hot summer days there is always a pleasant, refreshing breeze at sea. The night sea is calm, but during the daytime, the coming and going of yachts and dinghies disturbs the peace, creating annoying waves. Just behind the dock on the small square, you can find a well-stocked grocery store selling good quality fresh fruit and vegetables that are hard to resist.

After a short walk up you will reach a large square where there is a good supermarket selling just about everything. It even delivers your purchases free of charge, directly to your craft.

When you make a sizeable purchase, the grocery store owner treats you to an unexpected and complimentary gift such as fresh or dried fruit, and even if you buy less he throws in a handful of pistachios with a wink. But all the villagers in Göcek are very kind and friendly, and we are always happy to go back.

I suggest provisioning for a full week if you intend to sail into Skopea Bay, because in the next anchorage the bays are wonderful, but apart from a small fisherman's restaurant, they are deserted.

The promenade gives you a chance to buy nice souvenirs and Turkish handicrafts like ceramics, hand-woven carpets, or items of jewelry. Fish or meat is available in every restaurant. On the square behind the docks there is a big restaurant, easy to locate on account of its fish pond in the garden at the entrance. In the pond you can often see big grouper swimming.

Cheaper, but just as good, is the restaurant along the main street that runs parallel to the waterfront. This one you can pick out thanks to its oriental furniture, rich carpets, and cushions, where you can dine out in Turkish style, sitting on pillows around a short wooden table. The speciality of the house is grilled meat, but I tried out the grilled fish and it was excellent too. To end the soirée, or just for a snack, "Dr. Jazz" is a nice place with good music that can be found as you walk along the waterfront by the moorings of wooden boats for day trippers.

The public dock can be contacted by tuning in to VHF channel 16. The daily price for a 50-ft. yacht is $50 including water and electricity.

To moor at the public dock you have to drop anchor, whereas in other marinas there are mooring buoys. For repairs, it is better to sail to Fethiye.

Diesel and gasoline are available by the can at the gas station on the large square by the supermarket.

In the bay, the red floating barge is the gas station where boats can moor to refill their fuel tanks, but of course the price per liter there is much higher compared to the ones on land.

Other marinas in Göcek
www.portgocek.com
www.gocekmarina.net
www.turkeyclubmarina.net
www.cnmarinas.com

CLEOPATRA'S BAY (36°38'.5N 28°51'.3E)
This is one of my favorite anchorages, but every year larger gullets and smaller day-tour vessels arrive, packed with Northern European tourists in tiny swim suits. Luckily, these boats leave around 11 a.m. for another bay. This beautiful little spot, in any case, is just ten miles away from Göcek and not to be missed. The crystal clear blue waters are deep up to just a few feet from shore and flanked by tall cliffs covered with emerald green pines.

You have to drop the anchor in fifty feet of water and attach the stern line to special bollards that are now fixed ashore because tying ropes around the trunks of pines is forbidden in the bay. The afternoon is the best time to swim among the ruins, which, due to bradyseism, are now partly sunken. From the cliff you can see all of the old building, which is probably what remains of a Byzantine church.

The name of the bay originates from the legend that reckons it was a meeting place for Cleopatra and Marc Anthony when they were planning to take over this region of the Roman Empire.

The bay is situated in very attractive surroundings, and it is possible to go for a walk and get completely absorbed in nature. Don't forget to bring your camera because from the hills and the clifftops, the view is breathtaking.

At a walking distance, just across the bay, is Wall Bay offering a similar yet larger anchorage, without the sunken ruins. In this bay there is a wooden pontoon that has been built by the waterfront restaurant owner. Usually, it is free, but then they expect you to dine at the restaurant, which is clean, with very friendly staff. The speciality of the house is an entire lamb spit-roasted in a pine wooden fire, nothing short of delicious! The prices are reasonable and it is a magical spot.

TOMB BAY (36°41'.8N 28°52'E)

Tomb Bay is situated six miles from Cleopatra's Bay. There is a nice anchorage, well protected from the prevalent summer winds.

You can lower your anchor on the east side of the solid rock cliff where some ancient tombs are cut out from the rock, or moor at the small wooden dock or mooring buoy in front of the small restaurant.

The beautiful natural scenery is enhanced by the small tombs that for centuries have been an integral part of this bay. Starting from a tiny spring, close to the cliff, a winding rivulet flows down to a reddish gravel beach. All around as far as the eye can see, wooded hill after wooded hill stretches to distant high azure-colored mountains, which disappear into the horizon.

The green seawater is pristine and swimmers will notice it feels cooler as they get closer to shore. An easy enough walk up the cliff to look at the tombs presents you with an incredible view on the bay and a chance to take beautiful photos of your yacht anchored down below.

In this bay there are two restaurants where you can go for dinner or just to relax at sunset and drink an icy Raki. If you stop for dinner, try the chicken or fish Kebab and the great French fries which are handcut by the owner's wife—forget the frozen potatoes served elsewhere.

One day is not enough to fully enjoy a place like this.

TERSANE (36°40'.65N 28°54'.9E)

This small, practically deserted island is only three miles from Tomb Bay. Tersane can no doubt be regarded as one of the safest and most beautiful anchorage spots on the Turkish coast.

A narrow inlet channel flanked by gray rocks leads to the tiny, unique bay that seems like a sort of lake. The anchorage is well protected in all weather conditions. The prevailing atmosphere is one in which time seems to have stopped long ago. Ashore, patches of olive trees and undisturbed tufts of palm trees grow among big gray rocks. Nothing else is found here except for a family who lives on the island and in the summer runs a small waterfront restaurant. At the very end of the bay, the Byzantine ruins of a tiny church stand near the seashore, with some other ruins further away.

The sea water is green and not azure, but it is clean and calm as a pool, and you are tempted to dive into it from the boat. This bay is so well protected from the wind that in summer it's warmer than other anchorages. The wind rarely blows here: even when gusts perturb the inner channel, the bay is only touched by a light breeze.

When inside this rounded bay you can drop the anchor in twenty feet of water. The muddy bottom has some rocks and provides a good hold. As usual you must fix a line ashore.

At night, the restaurant, fringed by tufts of palm trees waving in the wind, is lit by a green light, and its reflection illuminates the whole area making it seem surreal.

The simple cuisine here offers a few dishes that are cooked in a wooden oven. All the meat comes from the animals that live on this small island. Sometimes even the fish is freshly caught. But in this restaurant, the meat cooked in the oven and seasoned with a secret blend of spices is better than the fish!

Wild donkeys, mules, and goats roam the stony, gently sloped hills undisturbed and are a common sight, especially in the hottest hours when they are found in the shade of ancient olive trees.

BOYNUZ BUKU (NO GPS POSITION)

Boynuz Buku anchorage is only a couple of miles away from beautiful, uninhabited Tersane Island.

Terta, a big rock, emerges from the middle of the cobalt sea, just in front of the bay's entrance. At the very end of the deep creek is one of the best sheltered anchorage spots. There is no particular danger in sailing to the end of the bay, and navigation is free of impediments. The anchor is dropped in twenty-five feet of water and its muddy bottom offers a secure hold. The north and south side of the bay are completely carpeted with pine trees and at the end of the anchorage area there is a hardwood forest, while near the shore, pink and white oleanders grow. The creek is bordered by thick woods and luxuriant vegetation, reminiscent of a mountain lake. The calm, clean, green seawater also happens to be as cold as lake water.

Ashore, freshwater is available to refill the water tanks and there is a restaurant that serves a good meal under the shade of pine trees.

Skopea Limani has an array of what seems like never-ending safe and beautiful anchorages, like Amazon Bay, Wall Bay, "22 Fathoms Bay," and many other bays that can be only day anchorages like the nice one in between the tiny Yassica Islands.

We now leave this unique sailing area and head to the open sea in the huge Fethiye Corfezi Gulf, our course southbound.

As soon as you round Cape Ilbis, the big bay of Gemiler appears. It is renowned for two striking anchorages, and for its famous white sandy beach at the Olu Deniz blue lagoon.

KARACAOREN BAY (NO GPS POSITION)

After twenty miles of navigation from Boynuz Buku you reach the bay. Though not very well protected from the sea, it is nonetheless absolutely unique. In following a logical course that leads to Gemiler Island from the Cape of Ilbis, you pass near this anchorage, which is great for spending a night if the sea is calm and you have time.

The tiny rocky island that is full of Byzantine ruins is called Karacaoren, also the name of this bay. Be very careful when approaching this anchorage because there are many rocks lying just a few feet under the water's surface. I therefore suggest approaching it through the north channel.

The best shelter for anchorage is on the southerly side, at the very end of the bay. Here the restaurant's staff is available to assist with mooring. In fact, the restaurant perched on the high cliff that overlooks the bay has a young man on a dinghy to help fix the stern mooring line ashore. When you are anchored, dive into the crystal clear water and check that the anchor post is adequate for your boat, and then just relax and enjoy the beauty of this place. Here the sea is irresistible and great for snorkeling since you can see some fragments of Byzantine pottery on the *seafloor*. Do not try to take any of the pieces, not even a single one, for Turkish officials are extremely strict in such cases.

A restaurant sits on an outcropping of rock, thirty feet above the sea. The meals are excellent and the service is good. You will find ready-to-eat hors-d'oeuvres and the main course is cooked in a distinctively shaped, big wooden oven. The homemade bread is delicious and the family that runs the restaurant is very hospitable. At dinner, the father starts playing the violin at a certain time, entertaining guests and then he passes by the tables, serving glasses of Raki to finish the meal.

The cost per person is thirty dollars, including the transfer on the dinghy to and from your vessel to the restaurant.

GEMILER (NO GPS POSITION)

Karacaoren is just one sea mile from the famous island of Gemiler. Anchorage is in the narrow channel between the mainland and the rocky island. The water is very deep and you must drop your anchor in fifteen or sixteen feet of water. The muddy sea ground is a good holder, and it rises quickly only a few feet from shore. In this anchorage, too, you must secure a stern mooring rope to shore.

Generally, it is no problem finding help for this job since there are many young boys waiting around near the anchorage aboard tiny boats with powerful outboard engines, ready to help cruisers. For these young people, helping sailors is an excuse to try selling their ice cream or renting jet skis, or for offering parasailing, or even to propose a romantic dinner at a restaurant on the sandy beach. If you intend to dine at a restaurant, the kids come to pick you up by boat when you are ready.

Gemiler attracts tourists from all over the world, thanks to its unique charm. Centuries-old wild olive trees grow from the rocks and sit next to old Byzantine villages that have been abandoned for centuries. Former inhabitants had to leave this territory due to bradyseism. For this same reason, underwater, and from the deck of your boat, you can observe the perimeter of the Byzantine houses, and swim above the ruins. The exceptional transparency of the sea lets you see more than seventy feet below.

A small entry fee must be paid to visit the island. The tickets are sold at the entrance of the archaeological site located on the south side of the island, near the channel anchorage.

It's exciting to walk along ancient pathways that are sometimes stone paved. The original beauty of the remains of the church have been preserved, including its mosaic floor, but to see it, you must be very lucky, because to protect this authentic masterpiece from the deterioration caused by atmospheric agents, the archaeologists cover it with sand when they aren't working on the site. Note that samples of the mosaic floor can be found in Turkish and also in Japanese museums, because a Japanese archaeological team has been working for many years on the island.

In the summer season, this wonderful area is invaded by yachts and gullets, with dozens upon dozens of daily excursion trips departing from Fethiye and Göcek. Though these boats, which stop less than an hour in this unique anchorage, do spoil the fantastic atmosphere while they are there, it returns once they depart, making afternoons and night time magical.

From the top of the hill, the island offers an idyllic panorama of a cobalt blue open sea that stretches to the wild coast.

Only when it isn't peak season do I suggest visiting the famous and really beautiful white beach and the blue lagoon of Olu Deniz, just two miles from Gemiler. The Olu Deniz beach is where the sea turtle species called "Caretta-Caretta" builds its nest. In full season, the beach is jam-packed with multicolored beach umbrellas and tourists that end up spoiling the true beauty of this spot.

The Turkish authorities have banned anchorage in the lagoon. With a calm sea, it is possible to anchor close to the lagoon, near the warning notice.

Another nice anchorage is a mile northwest from Gemiler Island. A small bay provides good shelter in case of light winds. Here you can have greater privacy and visit the ruins by dinghy. At the end on the west side of this bay, clean, transparent water washes a small white shingle beach where you will find a tiny restaurant that prepares delicious dishes. A fresh water rivulet flows to the sea just below the high rocky cliff near the beach. Swimming in this bay, you sometimes come across a current of very cold fresh water that, like a river in the sea, flows deeper beneath the surface.

In this bay, an excursion boat stops daily and drops its anchor close to the cliff. One of the sailors onboard this tourist-filled vessel then climbs to the top of the rocky cliff and dives into the sea in grand style, like the famous Brazilian divers of Rio de Janeiro.

FETHIYE (36°37'.4N 29°06'.2E)

The approach to this large bay is not dangerous or difficult during the day.

Big white concrete buildings stand out against the green of the surrounding pine forest. When you see the island of Fethiye, pay attention since the water is shallow. You should therefore follow the coastline, keeping a distance of at least three hundred feet from the shore.

A beacon, called Battikaya, marks the limit of this dangerous shallow water.

As you enter, on the right, you can see an elegant tourist resort called Letoonia that has a rather big private marina where mooring for yachts in transit is possible.

Approaching the port, you will see a concrete wharf of about three hundred feet where big yachts or small cruising ships can be berthed, and from which some hydrofoils connecting Fethiye with the Greek island of Rhodes depart and arrive.

The public dock is designated to give hospitality only to the large caiques and other boats flying the Turkish flag.

Very close by, west of the public dock, there is a new marina where mooring is possible.

This new structure can berth many boats on the floating pontoons and offers all yachting services.

The marina also has assistants on board dinghies who assign the berth and help during the mooring.

The price per night, for a 50-foot boat, is about 60 dollars.

Port Facilities

Electricity, water, mooring, all services for engine repairs, carpenter jobs and stainless steel work—just ask the marina office. Diesel is available on the dock from a tank truck.

A ship chandlery is at walking distance from the marina.

The wooden jetty of the small hotel near the marina can be an alternative choice.

Ten boats with their own anchor in 25 feet of water can

be moored on this T-shaped dock. The bottom is mud and therefore provides a good hold for anchors.

The owner's daughter usually assists with mooring maneuvers and provides information about where the 220 volt plug and the connection for the water are to be found.

She even gives a warm welcome and invites the crew to swim in the swimming pool that is close to the pontoon, and is included in the mooring fee.

The toilet and hot shower facilities are very clean.

The restaurant, in a peaceful place near where the yachts are moored, prepares simple dishes at a good price.

The price per night for a 50-foot boat is about 35 dollars.

There are two similar pontoons out in the bay, further away from the town.

At the end of the bay, a small shipyard can host a few boats in 30 feet of water with a muddy bottom that is a very good holding ground.

The anchorage is safe and comfortable. You can reach land by tender and padlock it to the hotel pontoon or directly on a concrete wharf in the town close to the local fishermen's boats.

The town is lively and pleasant, and in its historic center there are inexpensive restaurants that prepare excellent grilled fish. Fresh fish is exhibited on an ice bed to show its quality.

I suggest tasting the shrimp, or chicken "casserole" cooked in a wood oven.

In the town you find a couple of the big supermarkets that are stocked with lots of European products, and which deliver, free of charge, directly to the boat.

I found that the most fully stocked supermarket is in Tanzas, close to the post office.

Be sure not to miss the Lycian tombs perched in the rocks that dominate the town. On the way there, you will encounter some very big, old stone sarcophagi.

One of the many anchorages in the Bay of Fethyie

A Roman theater sits at a busy crossing behind the long concrete wharf.

A climb will get you to the ancient theatre, where you can catch a glimpse of the high wall of the Knights' fortress.

The old fortress still preserves the ancient houses, which were not destroyed by the devastating earthquake of 1957, and has a maze of streets inside with a plethora of shops selling local handicrafts, fake designer clothes, pottery, and very fine carpets.

Remember to always negotiate the price.

Another must-see is the market close to the old town.

Inside the building, you will find a rich and vast array of fresh fruit and vegetables, as well as a fish and meat market.

GENERAL INFORMATION

Ideal for

It's a pleasure to sail in this area, even for sailors who are just starting out. The Fethiye Bay is a good sea to practice on since the wind conditions are never extreme, and the sea may often be choppy but is very rarely rough. The sea area that stretches from Ekincik to Kurdoglu Cape, on the other hand, can be demanding when the meltemi wind blows strong. During the winter season there are more chances to have a southerly storm, and in that case navigation in the open sea can be dangerous because of high waves.

In high season, especially July and August, anchorages and the marinas can be crowded because many pleasure-boaters are attracted by the beauty of this area. But there are several hundred anchorages in this fantastic Turkish area, so the region can host all sailors.

Weather

A long warm summer-like season lasts from April through the end of November, giving sailors the opportunity to enjoy plenty of dry, warm Mediterranean weather.

July and August are the months the meltemi wind blows and it can blow for days on end, very strongly. Compared to the Carian Coast, the Lycian Coast is less affected by the meltemi wind, and the bays of Fethiye and Skopea are well protected so that the wind is always more gentle there than it is in the open sea.

In the summer season, rain is very unusual. Note that in the harbor of Fethiye some summer days can be very humid.

Spring and autumn are the best months to visit this unique area, thanks to gentle, warm sea breezes and long sunny days.

Reference Pilot Books

We sailed these waters using *Turkish Waters and Cyprus Pilot*, by Rod Heikell, published by Imray.

Navigation Rules

Along the entire Lycian Coast there are no restrictions, with the exception of Karaagac Bay, a bay close to Marmaris Bay that is a military area. In this bay, navigation is forbidden.

Connections

Dalaman International Airport is the closest airport in the area. The town of Fethiye or the village of Göcek can be reached from there by bus or taxi. The distance from Dalaman airport to the town of Fethiye is 55 miles, and in 2008 the taxi fare is 80 dollars. From Dalaman airport to Göcek, the distance is 25 miles and the taxi fare is 40 dollars.

A couple of hydrofoils depart weekly, linking the Greek island of Rhodes and Fethiye. The taxi station is close to the concrete wharf in Fethiye Harbor and, in order not to have any nasty surprises, you should read the notice posted there listing taxi fares to some of the most popular destinations.

Distances

Marmaris – Ekincik:	28 miles
Ekincik – Skopea (lighthouse in Peksimet island):	30 miles
Göcek – Cleopatra's Bay:	10 miles
Cleopatra's Bay – Tomb Bay:	6 miles
Tomb Bay – Tersane Island:	3 miles
Tersane Island – Boynuz Buku:	3 miles
Boynuz Buku – Karacaoren:	23 miles
Karacaoren – Gemiler Island:	1 mile
Gemiler Island – Fethiye:	28 miles

Web Sites

www.lycianturkey.com

www.turkishclass.com to download Turkish dictionary software.

www.gocekyachtclub.org

PART 3

The Lycian Coast: From Fethiye To Antalya

Kalkan

A bright summer day, with a crisp blue sky and warm, dry air, greeted us that morning.

It was a day like many other sunny days in the Mediterranean—yet the air had a certain refreshing feel that somehow made the day feel like a special one. Our hearts were filled with a sense of optimism, and our bodies with an exuberant physical energy, which put us in a very good mood.

In fact, we very often wake up feeling full of positive energy, with a sense of joy that prompts a smile at the simplest things—for instance, just knowing that it is going to be another beautiful day to live to the fullest, savoring every hour.

This happiness sheds a positive light on everything, even the most banal things, and helps you to live in harmony with the perennial conflict between your (many) induced needs and your true needs (very few, actually).

In our case, since all day long we lived in a bathing suit and T-shirt and had practically no other needs, it was easy to forget about a structured lifestyle and conspicuous consumption.

We had a large breakfast in the morning. It consisted of milk and homemade, freshly baked bread, which was delivered to JANCRIS' deck wrapped in a newspaper. It was brought to us by a young man in a red boat.

We covered our slices of fragrant bread with the pine honey we had bought at the market of Fethiye. The taste was so delicious that we ate more than usual.

Just outside the companionway, a red straw basket contained the objects that needed to be kept handy–our sunglasses and tanning cream, with a protection factor of 8, which we applied every morning as we stuck our noses out.

The moment that he noticed that there was some movement on board, the young man would row his boat toward JANCRIS without turning the engine on, to earn his bread money.

Since he probably understood that we were still in bed, he left the bread on the boat but made sure not to wake us up. He then hung around to get paid. A nice boy and he was truly discreet!

As I paid him, I asked him to release the floating line at stern, which I recovered while Nicoletta weighed the anchor.

The boy, standing on his boat, waved goodbye with his muscular arms; we did the same and caught the last glimpse of the wonderful island of Gemiler which became smaller and smaller at the stern.

After navigating with the engine on for some miles, we neared Cape Kotu and there found the meltemi wind, which was great for hoisting the sails and the jib at the mizzen since the wind was astern.

When running with the wind, we rarely hoist the mainsail because it would take the wind away from the jib, which in turn would end up slacking. In hoisting the mizzen jib we have more space between the sails, enabling the jib to fill up, to gain speed and stability.

The sea we were sailing on is generally known as the "Seven Capes." It is notorious for its meltemi wind, which creates violent gusts as it descends from the rocks, and high waves that make for a stormy sea.

On our south-southeast course, navigation was smooth, pleasant, and fast, as we were running with the wind; we certainly did not envy those sailboats that were heading north, with their sails reefed, forced to smash against each wave, the bow jumping up to fall back again.

"These boats must have left Kalkan before dawn, to be here now," said Nicoletta, pointing to a group of four sailboats that had crossed our course, sailing close-hauled against the sea and wind.

"I think so, and they did well to be off so early," I replied, adding, "This way, at least half of their journey will be powered by the engine since they will have no wind and waves to slow them down. Today's meltemi appeared at around nine this morning and won't diminish until tonight."

"When northbound again, on our return trip, we really ought to wake up very early to avoid a demanding close-hauled sail that lasts hours," concluded Nicoletta. She then went to stern to see the boats cross our slipstream. Onboard, the crew, who were looking at us and waving, had brightly colored oilskins on to protect themselves.

Early in the afternoon, we reached the peaceful water of the deep bay of Yali Limani. The charming little town of Kalkan encompasses a well-protected port, located on the northeastern tip of the bay.

As we approached, the wind dropped and we had to lower the sails and turn the engine on.

Low white houses were clearly visible on the hills, beyond the tall sea wall that protects the inner waters, while the homes and restaurants below remained hidden from sight until we reached the small but bustling port.

The dock west of the port is assigned to vessels in transit or to private ones; the eastern side, on the other hand, is intended for all sorts, sizes, and types of boats for daily excursions or diving.

On land, a man was waving to attract my attention. My first response was to wave back, but then I noticed that he was pointing to a berth slip. He placed himself there, his legs well planted and arms ready to help us maneuver, and waited for us to swing our mooring lines over to him so he could secure them to the bitts on the cement dock.

Nicoletta, from the prow, observed the anchor swinging a few inches from the bow. Ready to drop it into the water, she had tied the fenders in their place; the lines at stern were coiled, and ready to be thrown to the man on land.

Though the port was roughly 150 feet long, the many boats that were moored there were cramped in and painstaking attention had to be paid when maneuvering.

Once moored, we found on land all the comforts and services of a well-equipped port: the chance to hook up to electric power and have freshwater, which in the last three weeks, since we were anchored in small bays, we'd had to do without.

Not that it was much of a sacrifice: JANCRIS has an efficient desalinator that supplies seventeen gallons of great freshwater per hour, and there are a number of alternative systems in place onboard to meet our needs for electric power. We have two 53-watt solar panels, and on the mizzen mast, around the spreader, we installed a powerful wind generator; both are powered by JANCRIS' service batteries.

Less ecological, but still very useful, is the 3.5 kW main generator, located in the engine chamber. It generates 220 volts of electric power, just like at home.

By using technology intelligently, we can not only be autonomous but also navigate safely and have a bit of extra comfort—small priceless luxuries like sipping a cool beer on a hot sunny day, or listening to good music.

Naturally, primary sources of electric power and water need to be used sparingly, keeping conservation in mind. But this rule is not only true aboard ship, it should be applied generally, to preserve the environment's precious resources.

The village of Kalkan is simply superb. It is an ancient Greek village, which, after the earthquake of 1958, was partly restored. It now boasts a charming and fascinating labyrinth of little streets with souvenir boutiques selling local handicrafts.

From JANCRIS' bow, Nicoletta observed the streets, crowded with houses, a few of which had verdant terraces where restaurant tables were arranged, offering, in the evenings, a refreshing breeze along with a superb view.

Moving close to her I asked if she felt like going for a walk, to see the old village.

"Of course," she replied, adding, "I was just now looking at the town, and if I remember properly, four years ago there seemed to be fewer buildings on the hillside, but the port and the village seem the same."

"True," I answered, "and as we were entering the port, I saw a few new hotels built along the coast. They were certainly not here before. Even the semi-detached homes on the hills are new, but the landscape does not seem to have been spoiled, nor was the old citadel defaced."

"Great!" she exclaimed, as she headed for the cockpit, "After about eight hours of sailing, I would say that we truly deserve an invigorating shower and a pleasant walk."

The promenade leads to the opposite end of the port. As its parade of locals crosses your path, they smile to greet you and make you feel like less of an outsider.

The uphill road that leads to the historic town center

seems like a great bazaar and, at its feet, has some of the fanciest restaurants in the area.

Outside the restaurants "client hunters" attempt kindly, but often unsuccessfully, to get us to look at their menu and prices, to convince us to eat there.

A number of shops sell and display their carpets and artifacts. Since the goods are sometimes so unique and appealing, we cannot help but stop and admire the item, knowing full well that a man will soon appear to try and lure you into his shop.

Being no easy prey since we don't need souvenirs, we naturally try, without offending them, to let them know that they need not waste time on us.

What struck us about the village was to see how many real estate agencies had opened in this elegant small beach town over the years.

Recalling its Greek counterparts, the village was characterized by steep steps that alternated with light colored stone paved streets that were framed with a white contour. At twilight, an intense perfume of jasmine filled the late afternoon air and it lingered until eight in the evening.

From every open window, and from the shops, Arab music was playing; in some areas, the air was filled with a pungent and tangy aroma of smoke. It came from the hookah [water pipe], indicating the proximity of a café, where men spend their time sitting on tiny stools, smoking, chatting, and playing backgammon, noisily tossing chess pieces on the inlaid wooden board.

We returned to port to dine onboard JANCRIS. Kalkan proved once again to be the fascinating and beautiful village we remembered; only a little more crowded and lively, but always a hospitable place with kind inhabitants living their traditional lifestyle.

After dinner, we went back to have an ice cream. Seated at one of the tables in the café, which towers over the little port from above, we could keep an eye on our boat.

In the darkness of the evening, from our mooring, the village looked like a nativity scene, with its multicolored lights shining all the way up the hill.

The hills in the background were also lit with another extraordinary light—the full moon. Like the waves of a stormy sea, amber colored light glittered here and there from the small hamlets perched atop.

Around the port, the car traffic is almost nonexistent since the paved road ends at the port's entry, and very few cars, except for taxis, and supermarket delivery vans transporting food supplies, can access the area.

The port that sheltered us buzzed with music and life. The sounds permeated the air and reached our boat.

That morning, as I had planned, I washed the boat and all its accessories with freshwater, starting fore and aft.

To do things perfectly, the boat, after its final rinse, had its steel and chrome parts wiped dry. Concentrating on drying the central stanchions with my leather cloth, I went about my business when, out of the blue, a voice from land caught my attention.

It belonged to a perfectly shaved young man with well-groomed jet-black hair.

Standing next to JANCRIS' gangway, he was waiting for me to disembark and move toward him.

I did just that: I walked up to him and asked what he wanted.

"Captain," he said in a low voice and speaking excellent English, "have you ever seen the gully of Saklikent and the archaeological site of Xantos?"

"Xantos? Yes, I have," I answered, "but not the gully of Saklikent. Are you a taxi driver? Are you offering us an excursion?" I asked in a straightforward manner.

The boy instantly blushed and then said, "Yes, Captain. I have a taxi and I offer you a very special price to visit the gully. Half a day is all you need."

"Thanks, but we can't leave the boat."

Without even giving me time to politely end the discussion, he persistently continued in his low voice, "Please, Captain, I didn't work today. Come see the gully, you'll see that it is a beautiful place."

"All right," I replied, sighing. "Wait a minute though, I must ask my wife if she likes the idea," and I moved to the cockpit which leads below, and went in.

Nicoletta, the moment she heard me mention the gully of Saklikent, jumped with enthusiasm.

"It must be magnificent. Carla mentioned the place several times and said it's really worth seeing. Are we going now?" she asked, all excited.

"At this point I would say that the answer is a definite yes!" I answered and made my way up, to tell the young man the good news.

"You can call me Alì, captain."

We seemed to have made him happy. He rushed off and went toward his parked car.

Ten minutes later, we were seated in Alì's spotless and scented taxi, a Fiat 131 model made in Turkey.

The road ran along a narrow wooded gorge, past cultivated valleys and portions of land covered in greenhouses, which, like mirrors, reflected the implacable rays of the sun.

The impression I had of this land, which unfolded before my eyes from the backseat car window, was that it is a rich and bountiful land that requires farmers to toil but at the same time yields a satisfyingly rich harvest.

At a certain point, we got off the main road. We followed a secondary bumpier and winding road across a thick pine woodland and eventually the road turned into a very narrow dirt track.

Some miles down the road, there was a big parking lot.

A couple of restaurants were set there. They stretched over a vast surface crossed by streams, little cascades, ponds and spurting fountains, offering a sensation of freshness and absolute peace. Soft plush cushions had been placed around low tables that sat just above the ground on a surface paved with wooden boards, standing above the ponds.

"After the sightseeing, we'll eat here, right?" asked Nicoletta, already sure of the answer.

The driver, who would not leave us for even a second, understood Nicoletta's intentions and therefore booked a table. He said that while we visited the gully, he would wait for us here.

"Great," I answered, as we distanced ourselves from the restaurant and headed for the entrance of the gully, which had the omnipresent ticket office.

We paid for our tickets, and proceeded up a steep metal ladder, then walked along a makeshift boardwalk that flanked the steep granite rocks. For thousands of years these rocks have been sculpted by the running water, which has made their surface smooth, and has created deep furrows that at times can be some thirty feet deep.

The strong stream of the torrent flowed beneath our feet. When you looked up, amid the huge twisted branches of fig trees that emerged like spurs in the rocks, you could catch a glimpse of the azure sky, which recalled the summers in canyons.

The impressive walls that drop vertically, reach, in some points, heights that surpass three hundred feet and give you vertigo.

At a certain point, an ample cove opened, and we walked on big, smooth cobblestones, our legs in the icy cold water of the stream to get to the opposite bank.

From there, immersed in this fairytale scenery, we walked upstream, past walls excavated from the mountains, that were at times so close to each other that it makes you feel uneasy.

"Imagine how fast the water flows in spring here," said Nicoletta pointing up to a fissure in the rock, about one hundred and fifty feet deep and no wider than six feet. "Look up there—the water surely reaches the ledge, where that trunk is embedded. It must be at least sixty feet above our heads," she concluded with a mix of worry and amazement.

The view was truly breathtaking. The huge glossy gray tree trunk resembled a broken toothpick, stuck in the fangs of a monster.

Every nook and cranny offered sights that were unique; every polished, rounded rock resembled a sculpture of grotesque figures or monstrous animals.

Time ticked away quickly, and before we knew it, it was already time to get back.

Never would we have expected to see such wonderful things.

The gully of Saklikent is naturally majestic and truly memorable, so if you are lucky enough to be in the area, we strongly advise seeing it.

The Bay of Kekova

As we neared the very beautiful Greek island of Kastellorizon, an unexpected breeze started blowing which deceived us into hoisting the sails. So we went, with our mainsail hoisted, and our engine running as well.

Like true novices, our eagerness to sail—to live harmoniously in the silence of the sea and wind—had betrayed us.

To our disappointment, the bit of wind that had appeared and induced us to hoist the mainsail never came back. A little angry at ourselves for having given in to such a sailing mirage, we soon realized that the lack of wind in the area had been clearly evident.

Mile after mile, all around us the sea was as flat as a blue table, while the air, hazy and dense, was still, enabling us to see the horizon.

JANCRIS' bow rode the water, swinging over the white foam that glided along its immaculate sides and disappeared at the stern.

Scores of black rocks and islets, no larger than tennis courts, protrude from the center of the two-mile-wide strait that separates the Greek island from the Turkish coast. This makes navigation dangerous, even during the day.

The shores that outline the channel are tall and barren—a marked contrast with the cobalt blue of the sea.

JANCRIS, now piloted by the Simrad autopilot, glided speedily on the water as I sat aft to enjoy the view; Nicoletta was at the bow. She kept an eye on our course toward the western tip of the Bay of Kekova.

All of a sudden, a shiny gleam from the sea caught my eye. I stood up and moved closer to the side of the boat, and saw, just below the surface of the water, the clear profile of a dolphin diving in and out of the water as it headed for our bow.

Nicoletta had also noticed the company we had, so she moved to the bow quickly to watch the show.

Two or three dolphins were playfully swimming around us, and while keeping an eye on us, they plunged in and out of the wake produced by our bow.

They really seemed to enjoy their extraordinary underwater leaps and pirouettes that made them converge, then swerve swiftly to one side and finally plunge into the water; all truly amazing.

When they poked their heads out of the water to breathe, we tried to touch their smooth bodies but never managed to reach them.

Then, out of the blue, at the bow, a bigger and more self-confident dolphin emerged. Joining the others for a few seconds, it then went off, and the others followed, abandoning us.

From a distance, at intervals, we could see their silvery backs disappear into the open sea.

Our encounter, which lasted but a few minutes, had cheered us up; catching sight of dolphins always does. In an attempt to persuade them to come back, we rushed to the front, and we whistled, leaned out, and tried to establish contact with them. But then, once they were off for good, we watched their receding silhouettes with a little melancholy. We felt lonelier and less protected.

Though we have seen hundreds and hundreds of them, of all sizes and shapes, in all the seas around the world, catching sight of a dolphin has always proved to be a positive experience, one that cheers you up and makes your day a better one.

Even the memories related to the places where we saw dolphins are somehow different.

From the center of our bow we could see the island of Kekova clearly.

The amount of boat traffic, especially the caiques, is notable near the entrance to the inlet.

I went to the cockpit, slowed down, and then went back to the mast to help Nicoletta take down the full batten sail.

To lower a full batten sail is an easy, simple and fast operation thanks to the "lazy bag," the sail cover that is permanently mounted on the boom. The lacing at mid boom also prevents the sail from being blown overboard, and helps to neatly enclose the sail in a sack.

All that is needed is to furl the sail and zip it up—that's it.

The entrance to the rocky isles of Karaool Adalari and Kekova was well protected. We had realized that immediately and the calmness of the sea within confirmed our perception.

The Bay of Ucagiz was our destination. A true natural port, it is not only big but also well protected from all winds, so you can anchor easily and forget about the boat.

Unfortunately, the water in the bay, though clean, is green and murky, and not particularly inviting to swim in.

We headed to the western side of the bay and moored not far from the humble village of Ucagiz, near another five or six boats.

We immediately readied our dinghy, with its outboard

engine, to explore the area and seek more inviting and transparent water for swimming.

Our Yamaha engine switched on the first try without any problem. While we rode away from JANCRIS, I thought how great the engine really was. We had bought it, cheaply, on the island of St. Lucia, in the Caribbean, from the Yamaha dealer in Castris.

I couldn't wait to get rid of the old outboard. Pulling the starting rope to turn it on always had me out of breath, sweating and cursing. Then, the moment I was angry enough, "brumm," the engine would start.

So I placed a very visible notice at the stern of JANCRIS, announcing that the old engine was on sale.

And indeed, in a matter of a few days, to my great pleasure, a potential buyer, a young Rasta fisherman who was from St. Lucia, appeared.

He wanted to pay the established amount, two hundred dollars, in "weed," which was cultivated in the forest.

Such an unexpected proposal amused me and I answered that indeed, I wanted the green stuff in return, but I only accepted "classic green"—U.S. dollars, nothing else.

He finally paid, in dollars, but he seemed amazed by the thought that I had turned down his proposal. Still, off he went, carrying the more than 80 lbs of engine on his shoulder as if it were a feather.

After a few minutes of surfing the water, we reached the tiny beach that hems the Bay of Tersane.

A few small boats had moored, dropping their anchors, in the beautiful water of this bay.

Because of its small size, we took our dinghy straight to shore and lifted it out of the water.

Around the beach lay several ruins, hidden among the olive trees. The scene culminated in a great enigmatic arch that had somehow withstood time, and rests just a stone's throw away from the beach.

"The arch is wonderful!" said Nicoletta, moving closer

to it, "look, you can still see fragments of its colored frescoes. It must have been an old Byzantine cathedral," she concluded as she walked around the base of the arch.

To refresh myself, I dipped into the water. With the water shoulder deep, I turned around and looked behind me to discover that, all around, many more ruins than had appeared at first sight were strewn there.

It was very similar to Gemiler Island, where ancient buildings lay submerged below the bay.

"It's a pity there are so many boats here," I said to Nicoletta, who had by then decided to join me in the water. "It would be lovely to moor JANCRIS in this splendid bay." I hadn't even finished uttering these words when another wooden boat, one devoted to daily tourist excursions, with about ten guests, its keel touching the bottom, dropped its anchor practically on the beach.

"We'd better just swim and then go back to our boat," said Nicoletta before putting her face in the water and swimming away from the beach.

Sarcophagus in the well protected water in front of Castle Koy Island, Kekova

On our way back to JANCRIS, we took a little detour to-ward the picturesque village at the foot of the castle in the Bay of Kale Koy.

The many rocks and sandbars around the anchorage obliged us to keep our engine running at minimum speed to avoid any semi-submerged obstacles found near the shore. Then, we spied, in the middle of the water, a fascinating sar-cophagus, partly submerged in the center of a rocky inlet.

To prevent the propeller from touching the bottom, I turned the engine off, and pulled it up. I then jumped into the knee-deep water and pulled the dinghy close to the mysteri-ous stone sarcophagus, which just happens to be one of the most famous local sites, immortalized on all the postcards.

And indeed, the spectacular setting that has hosted it for centuries makes this attraction truly worthy of its fame.

The crenelated walls of the castle, running along the steep hillside, lend the place a unique charm and sense of mystery unlike any other. It may be because of the sea, or because of the rocks which, carved like steps, ascend from the water toward nonexistent houses, or due to the rugged-ness of the terrain. But, in all, this mix makes the inlet of Kekova a singular, incredible, and untamed place.

Very gradually, unable to take our eyes off this land, we moved on, trying to absorb and impress into memory as much as we could, to capture everything that Kastel Koy had to offer.

"I'd like to come back tomorrow to take pictures and film the spot," I said to Nicoletta.

"Wow," she said cheerfully, "you seem to have read my mind. Tomorrow when on land, we'll climb to the top of that hill. No doubt the view from up there is astounding," she concluded, gripping the handle of the dinghy tightly since its powerful engine made it rear over the water.

With dinnertime approaching, we sat in the cockpit to enjoy a Campari and orange juice. (A mariner's life is a hard one!)

A sailboat pulled silently into the bay, its bow pointing our way. "They want to moor here," said Nicoletta, as she watched them draw closer and closer.

"I have a feeling that we have seen the boat before," she added moments later, as it moved in even closer. "Its hull design seems familiar. . . . Of course, it's INTERMEZZO—Rod and Bernie, our South African friends!" We both sprang to our feet and greeted them.

They too had recognized JANCRIS and edged in just a few feet from our stern.

Rod, with her dark and ever-perfect hair, looked as though she'd just walked out of a beauty parlor. Donning a wide smile, she asked Nicoletta how we were doing.

Bernie, with very little fair hair left, and a pale, freckly complexion, was steering with one hand and waving with the other.

Their anchor was dropped near JANCRIS, like in the old days, when for a few months we roamed the northern Turkish coast together.

"Since it's dinnertime, why not invite them for some pasta?" proposed Nicoletta, "If I remember correctly, they both love spaghetti with carbonara sauce."

"I'd like that," I replied, and got on the dinghy to invite them over.

They gladly accepted our invitation. Bernie, who had been hoping all along that our routes would cross, said that he had bought some excellent South African wine in Johannesburg, with us in mind.

"You can't imagine how difficult it was for us to bring the twenty bottles of wine, which are now stowed away, all the way from South Africa on the plane, but the moment I tried the wine, I told Rod that Alfredo really must taste it since he's one of the few people we know who would truly appreciate it," he admitted, laughing. They arrived on their dinghy, tied it to a bitt at stern, and came onboard JANCRIS just as the sun was setting.

Rod hugged me warmly and said, "You can't imagine how often I spoke about you when you were sailing around the world on your Millennium Odyssey adventure. Reading articles on the regatta brought tears to our eyes, and, at times, a bit of envy, too, that we were not there sharing the experience with you, or seeing those beautiful spots. Naturally, we were also a little worried about you—after all, you sailed in very dangerous areas infested with pirates who have become crueller and more desperate over time; and you have crossed oceans, which must not have been an easy or relaxing experience. Instead, after four years, here we are, once again together on board your beautiful boat, and I see you looking wonderful, and even JANCRIS is in tip-top shape. How time flies!" was her conclusion, accompanied by a deep sigh.

"For you, the years seem not to have passed at all—you haven't changed one bit," I replied, and proceeded to the cockpit seats.

Nicoletta, handing a glass of Campari to Rod, inquired, "Where are you coming from?"

"We spent a wonderful winter at the Kemer Marina and then flew back home for a couple of months, because—you know how it is—our parents are getting older, and though they are healthy and strong, they like seeing us. Then again, for us, getting off the boat for a while is not bad. Plus, keep in mind that when it is winter here in the Mediterranean, and the weather is cold and rainy, in South Africa it is summer, and the climate is fabulous.

"We must admit, though, that we love the Kemer Marina with its bustling social life and its many opportunities. We joined other couples living on board their boats and hired a bus, with the help of the marina staff, to organize fabulous excursions around Turkey. We spent about a week sleeping in simple hotels, touring the incredibly beautiful archaeological sites near Iran and Syria. And it was all very cheap. Even when we were aboard our boat, in the marina, there were always fun things to do, like Sunday lunchtime barbecues in the shipyard lot. Other times, we would dine out, in some of the restaurants around the town, paying only ten or twelve dollars per person.

"Then there were the lessons: an English couple, twice a week, offered English lessons; a French couple did the same in their language. Enzo and Cettina, your friends onboard their boat PIGRETTA, offered Italian cooking lessons, teaching the art of making pasta and cooking it just right—*al dente*, or to make gnocchi and homemade *tagliatelle*. A New Zealand couple had a sewing machine on their boat and they gave professional sewing lessons to teach people how to make curtains and porthole covers, and to repair broken or old sails. Time was spent doing all these wonderful things," she said enthusiastically. She concluded by saying, "Now we plan to sail north to Istanbul to spend the upcoming winter in that fascinating city." We then raised our glasses and toasted to our casual encounter, after years of not seeing each other.

Bernie, on the other hand, was extremely curious, and wanted to know all about what we had been doing.

At dinner, he never stopped asking questions about our circumnavigation around the world. He wanted a very detailed account of our sailing adventure—a sailor's dream—as he called it.

For us, it is always difficult to recount the story of those two years of life lived to the fullest. It wasn't just a vacation trip!

Travelling, to us, is an experience without end, which must continue as we journey through our lives, and, though we are now in the Mediterranean, next year we want to once again move on.

Our memories of the around-the-world tour do not come out in chronological order. A mix of anecdotes unfolds rationally from memory, that is, when we experience or see something, we associate it with a set of recollections. Hence a perfume, the color or feel of a wave, the dazzling glare of an immaculate beach, these trigger memories of adventures, friends, or some of the highlights of this extraordinary trip.

Bernie, though, was all wrapped up with my tales of big storms, the most beautiful places in the world, and technical information regarding equipment and sailing.

He asked the questions that I too had asked my friends before undertaking a circumnavigation, (two, in fact), or prior to crossing the Atlantic (many more times).

Nicoletta and I, when telling the stories of our journey, illustrate it in our own individual ways. We rarely answer a specific question with an equally precise reply. It's simply inconceivable for the two of us to think that in two years of sailing you'll never encounter a storm.

Stories about storms will never convey the suffering and the hardship that hour upon hour and day after day of sailing entail; or the experience of days on end without having the physical possibility to have a warm meal or even go to the bathroom. The waves that range anywhere from twelve to thirty feet don't scare you when you talk about them as you are comfortably seated in a marina. Pouring rain that blinds you and stings your skin, or waves that invade the deck with the force of a flooding river—how can they really be perceived when you talk about them in a dry, warm, and cozy dining area?

These elements are inextricable parts of the game. Though you try to avoid them, sooner or later, they are bound to hit you, and when at sea, you take what you get.

Even the most beautiful places in the world resist classification. Everything depends on when you experience it, on the weather conditions. For instance, if you aren't lucky, you could be in the most beautiful place, but in the rain, with no sun, the place will no longer be a paradise, for its colors will be dull, and its azure water lead colored.

The Fiji islands illustrated this point for us: the week we arrived there, we had no sun in sight.

Fortunately, we spent three weeks there, and so had enough time to enjoy this marvelous place. But I can assure you that an atoll can seem abysmal in the rain and I'll go so far as to say that even the island's population seemed less friendly and open in bad weather. The sun makes everyone more cheerful, and in less of a rush. We, too, were different and more positive.

Having said this, I avoided talking any more about storms. Besides, our experience of storms was rare. I then listed for Bernie some of the places that had struck me most for their beauty: the Tuamotus and Vanuatu in the Pacific, Thailand, and the Maldives in the Indian Ocean.

Nicoletta, on the other hand, had the French Polynesian islands, and the coral reef in Australia with Lizzard Island, topping her list as some of the most enchanting places. But she also liked Malaysia, Thailand, and even Bali, she added.

"And in terms of nature," Nicoletta went on, "the Galapagos in the Pacific, and Sri Lanka in the Indian Ocean . . ."

Rod looked at Bernie who, in listening to our travel tales, had a dreamy expression on his face.

"There we go," said Rod smiling sarcastically at Nicoletta. "My man is off. He's gone for the next few days with his dreams of sailing the atolls in the Pacific Ocean and Australia. As if this were a bad place. Our problem is that since we purchased the boat in Antalya, and despite our flag at the stern, we have left South Africa. Our intention, one day, is to return home by boat, but this part of the world is so beautiful that we never leave," she said as though she were excusing herself.

"Rightly so," intervened Nicoletta. "The sea between Greece and Turkey is renowned for being one of the most impressive and interesting in the world. Though we were certain of this even before sailing around the globe, now that we have, and with our greater experience, we have returned to these waters with unfaltering certainty and can affirm that the Aegean is a true paradise for anyone who loves sailing."

By the time we got on deck, it was the middle of the night. Time truly flies when telling stories and listening to friends' tales.

We headed to stern where our dinghies were secured.

With the seawater perfectly still, the dinghies floated like two ducks. A light warm breeze came from the land. It carried a blend of scents that combined the smell of sun drenched Mediterranean vegetation with the pungent aroma of goat dung.

In the sky, a crescent moon shone majestically in the distance, lying low on the horizon.

"Look," said Nicoletta pointing toward it, "it looks like the crescent on the Turkish flag."

We watched the moon a little longer, and then Bernie and Rod got on their white dinghy and returned to their boat INTERMEZZO. Though silent as an engine can be, their outboard shattered the peace that had reigned over the entire bay.

Our eyes followed them, as they slowly disappeared into the distance, leaving a slight ripple on the black surface of the sea. One last time, they turned to wave goodbye to us, and we returned their salute, as we sat down on deck.

Bewitched by the silence and the magical night we were no longer tired.

We could feel the teak deck we were lying on absorbing the humidity as we gazed intently at the pulsing firmament of the sky.

"A shooting star," I pointed out, thrilled.

"I hope you made your wish," said Nicoletta.

"Of course," I answered, "I would like to live like this, free and in harmony, for a long time to come."

GUIDE FROM FETHYIE TO ANTALYA

Fethiye, Kalkan, Kas, Kekova, Finike, Tekirova, Kemer, Antalya

The coastline of the Anatolian Peninsula is one of the most beautiful in all of Turkey. An eastbound course is highly recommended, as it is where the Aegean and Mediterranean Seas continue their run into Asia.

The uncontested king of the Aegean Sea, the meltemi wind, weakens from this point on, and the winds become variable and baffling.

Mother Nature, in this part of the Turkish coast, has been generous to the inhabitants, as evidenced by the plentiful fresh water that runs in sparkling streams to the sea and by the deserted beaches that are almost suffocated by rich vegetation. In this area, farmers appear to be leading a good life growing juicy fruits and flavorful vegetables.

The clean sea has fish and lobsters in abundance, and it branches out into what seems a labyrinth of islands, tiny islets, fjords and big bays like Kekova Bay. This area is well known by yachtsmen since it offers easy sailing conditions—with short distances, calm water, and good anchorages.

The Taurus mountain chain has contributed to making sure that nature is not touched and spoiled by the speculations of the building industry.

This expanse of sea is fun for sailing and great refreshing swims; but there are also great opportunities to visit incredibly rich archaeological sites ashore, like the very old Lycian sarcophagus that for many centuries has slept immobile under the shade of big, knotty olive trees. Or, sites like in the bay of Kekova where one Lycian sarcophagus appears from the shallow sea water in a tiny corner close to Kastel Koy Island. And more—

like the Roman theaters, Greek temples or Byzantine churches. In admiring the ruins, you can't help but wonder how all this has survived so long and has withstood the ravages of time and all sorts of human vicissitudes.

The best course to follow is to sail from Fethiye to Antalya. Along this cruise you will undoubtedly enjoy charming nights anchored in safe and tranquil bays, or comfortable berths in modern, full service marinas.

To charter a yacht for a pleasure and cruise the area, the best place to rent one is in Göcek Harbor where charter flotillas are moored, ready to grant you an unforgettable cruising experience.

FETHYIE AND GEMILER
See Part 2 pages 102 and 104

KALKAN (36°15'.17N 29°24'.9E)
The Fethiye Bay's southerly side is closed off by Cape Ilbis. When you've doubled it, you change course and head south. After forty miles of navigation, you approach the big bay of Kalkan. In the summertime, if your course is northbound, it is better to set sail before daybreak because the meltemi starts blowing at about 9 a.m. In this case you are best off motoring your way up along the coast so that you don't have to sail against the wind and the high waves. The wind's maximum force is at about five p.m. and then its speed diminishes hour by hour until it finally dies out at night.

It is best to sail three or four miles from the coast, where the sea is deeper, and the waves are more gentle. From the island of Gemiler, until you reach Kalkan there are no bays for shelter.

Within Kalkan Bay, the wind usually dies and you have to turn on your engine and motor to the anchorage or to the small harbor of Kalkan.

A picturesque village sits atop the hills on the east side of the bay and some elegant resorts are found around the narrow entrance to the harbor.

The concrete wharf on the high breakwater side is for yachts in transit. It is also a public marina offering all facilities. On the opposite side, the berths are dedicated to local vessels. This tiny harbor is packed with boats, so if you intend to dock here, plan an early arrival—it is best to get here by early afternoon.

In case you prefer the privacy and the quiet of an anchorage, a couple of miles north of the harbor, you can drop your anchor in thirty feet of water where the ground offers a good hold.

A stern mooring rope must be secured ashore when anchoring.

In this charming cove, if you are lucky, you can swim in transparent turquoise water with the Caretta Caretta sea turtle.

Port Facilities
This tiny harbor is well sheltered from the prevalent summer winds.

Electricity and water are available. A laundry service and hot showers are near the wharf.

To drop anchor in this busy harbor is no easy job, so pay attention to other chains and anchors before dropping yours.

Set in the heart of the fishermen's village, the spot is peaceful and still untouched by mass tourism.

Supermarket and grocery stores deliver your merchandise directly to the boat.

The price of the municipal marina is reasonable: a 50-foot yacht pays 35 dollars per day, including electricity and water—great quality drinking water.

Be sure not to miss
Kalkan unfolds around the tiny harbor that is surrounded by the towering Taurus Mountains.

Late in the afternoon, when a gentle breeze cools the air, it's an absolute must to take a walk up the narrow, winding road that twists to the hilltop. Beautiful old Greek and Ottoman buildings strewn with big fuchsia-colored bougainvilleas have been watching for years over this old town.

Souvenirs, fashion, and Turkish handicrafts shops; restaurants; traditional Turkish cafés—this village never stops surprising the cruisers who stop here. A one-day stay in Kalkan is too short a time to fully enjoy the place.

If you have time, rent a taxi for half a day and visit (be sure to negotiate the price beforehand) the lovely archaeological site of Xantos, only an hour drive from the marina. If you prefer a cooler atmosphere try visiting the mountains—the appealing gorge of Saklikent. Their natural settings and sublime beauty evoke powerful emotions.

Kalkan is less than a two-hour drive from Dalaman airport.

Kalkan is more than a four hours driving distance from Antalya airport.

www.kalkanturkey.com

KAS (36°11'.9N 29°38'.5E)

Ten miles of navigation separates Kalkan from Kas. When sailing to Kas, pay attention to the dangerous submerged reef and the rocks that in some cases are not marked, especially in the channel between the Turkish coast and the Greek island of Kastellorizon. At night, the scattered rocks and tiny islands make navigation here very dangerous.

In the daytime, the sun shines and reflects on the cobalt sea and the gray rocks glitter like jewels. This area is great fun to sail, as the sea is calm and there is a northeasterly wind blowing parallel to the coastline.

In Kas Harbor, the marina is always very busy. Here too, it is best to plan an early a afternoon arrival, in order to have a chance to find a dock in the marina.

The village of Kas is bigger and noisier than Kalkan, and if you prefer privacy and tranquillity I suggest dropping anchor in the deep bay a couple of miles east where the muddy ground makes for a secure hold. In case you want to visit the charming village, you need a good dinghy with a powerful outboard to cross the harbor.

There is also the possibility of anchoring in the tiny natural harbor of Megisti on the Greek island of Kastellorizon just three miles from Kas. Do not forget to change your courtesy flag. The atmosphere here is very different from that of the Turkish coast; it is reminiscent of the beautiful Dodecanese Islands. The language and the dishes are different, while the faces are the same. They look like the faces of people who live only three miles away, neighbors who were sometimes hated. For years now they have been coexisting peacefully and tourists and goods are exchanged daily.

Mooring at the Kas Marina requires you to drop your anchor. The very busy harbor is a walking distance from the old town, boasting plenty of restaurants and shopping opportunities.

Port Facilities
Electricity and water are close to the dock.

A good selection of supermarkets and grocery stores deliver free of charge to the port.

Maintenance services are available; most small problems can be repaired—just ask the man who passes by late in the afternoon to collect the payment for the dockage. The mooring fees are the same as those in the marina of Kalkan.

Be sure not to miss
From Kas Harbor a daily trip to the famous archaeological site of Myra, with its extremely well-preserved huge Roman theater, is easy to organize. Or you can see the unforgettable Lycian site of Xantos. This well-preserved site was the chief city of Lycia and features Lycian, Hellenistic, Roman and Byzantine ruins. Many of the most prominent artifacts that were removed from this site in the 19th century are now on display at the British Museum.

KEKOVA BAY (WEST INNER CHANNEL 36°10'.3N 29°50'.6E)
From Kas you have to sail for twelve miles before spotting the inner west channel that leads yachts to the large bay of Kekova.

The meltemi disappears after a few miles and a thermal wind appears. Most of the time it is just a light breeze that blows eastward following the coastline.

Kekova Bay is sheltered by a long, narrow island, parallel to the coastline. In this area there are many tiny islands, coves, and fjords that have been navigated for millennia thanks to the calm inner water and safe anchorages.

Any nook and cranny of this spectacularly beautiful and history-filled landscape is ideal for anchoring your yacht. Each anchorage can be a dreamlike setting, as, for instance, the tiny cove of Tersane where in the middle of the curved sandy beach stands an ancient arch, all alone. The arch to date still has traces of the old fresco that once must have covered all of the church ceiling and was destroyed.

In peak tourist season the spot is very busy with daily tourist trips coming and going from the anchorage. The propellers make the crystal turquoise water cloudy as sand is churned up from the seafloor. In the summertime it is therefore better to drop anchor just outside of this tiny bay, to have more privacy and less noise, and to enjoy the bay in the afternoon when the daily trips are finished and the beach once again becomes deserted and peaceful.

For a great swim and to catch a glimpse of the beauty of marine life, I suggest visiting the wild and deserted Karaloz Cove, south of Kekova Island. This well-protected anchorage overlooks the open sea, and its water is incredibly clear. Emerald pine trees and silver olive trees grow among smooth gray granite rocks and caress the calm seawater with their branches.

In good weather you can spend your days here and forget the rest of the world. Ashore there are no buildings or streets—only woods, the Mediterranean Sea and the music of bird songs.

What to see ashore
Kalekoy literally means "castle village." It is a very popular yachting destination. Its name derives from the small castle, built in the Middle Ages, that overlooks the bay from the hilltop.

At the foot of the hill, some tiny waterfront restaurants are found on floating pontoons, where boats can moor alongside. If you intend to spend a night in this charming spot and have dinner in a restaurant, it is best to moor at the pontoon because the depth of the sea is considerable. If you prefer to drop anchor, sail half a mile and cast anchor in the tranquil bay of Ucagiz. From there, you can visit Kalekoy by dinghy.

As you approach the shore, the most famous stone sarcophagus in the area appears to rise up from the shallow azure water some feet from the shoreline like a mirage—but it isn't, it's reality!

My tip here is to go ahead and make the effort to walk up the path that passes through a neighborhood of small, old, run-down houses. You will surely come across kids who follow you on your walk to the hilltop, trying to sell handmade knick-knacks and summer clothes. From the top, inside the castle, you can admire an extraordinary seascape, and as you look eastward be sure to catch a glimpse of the wild landscape that holds numerous scattered sarcophagi. The well-preserved castle wall encloses a tiny Roman theatre—it is said to be the smallest in the world. To visit the castle and walk through the ancient sarcophagi behind the castle, you have to pay a cheap entrance fee at the kiosk in front of the castle.

In all weather, the large Bay of Ucagiz is a natural harbor ideal for anchoring or docking on the long, wooden pontoons made by the owners of the fisherman's tavern on the seafront. Docking on the pontoons is usually free if you dine at the restaurant. Some pontoons have electricity since there is a long electrical cable that connects them to the restaurant; and even fresh water is sometimes available. This tavern offers ordinary, uninteresting dishes, and the price is not attractive either. If you want to dine out, try the east end of the village, adjacent to the police station and the taxi area. The speciality of the house is steamed crab with French fries or local fish, grilled.

The poor, tiny village is now beginning to have a little more tourism and some souvenir shops have opened. A small supermarket and two grocery stores are open every day in the village.

Before leaving Finike, the best place to stop and anchor is the Bay of Gokkaya, on the extreme east end of the Bay of Kekova.

If possible, it is best to drop the anchor at the very end, near the waterfront fisherman's restaurant, the only building in the area. Unfortunately, some nights each week, the restaurant turns into a music bar and can be very noisy, so you must either opt for an anchorage that is well sheltered and hear music all night long, or moor in a quieter place that is a little more exposed. In any case the sea ground is sandy and muddy, thus providing a good hold. In this case, when anchoring there is no need to secure a stern mooring rope ashore.

Be sure not to miss exploring every nook and cranny of this bay by dinghy, as each corner is a surprise, unveiling a tiny white sandy beach, warm turquoise water, ruins. . . .

FINIKE (36°17'.6N 30°09'.2E)

From the anchorage of Gokkaya in the beautiful bay of Kekova, after a twenty-mile sail, you approach the Finike Marina, a well-protected and modern marina built near the village with the same name.

The town is neither charming nor interesting, but it is the orange capital of Turkey. The marina offers full services and is a good stopover when sailing to Antalya.

The safe Setur Marina can be a perfect place to leave the yacht and to go by car or taxi to visit the magnificent sites inland.

When approaching the marina, you must call the marina office by VHF on Channel 73 for docking assistance. You will quickly have a berth number and a dinghy leading you to the berth, and assisting you with the mooring buoy.

After several nights spent at anchor in the charming Kekova Bay, docking in a marina allows you to take advantage of all the services and to reorganize and tidy up your boat again.

Finike is well connected to Antalya and to the airport, so it is a good place to change crew.

The marina is adjacent to a yard equipped with an 80-ton travel lift and spacious boat parking where you can leave your vessel on the hard all winter long or just long enough to renew the antifouling treatment.

Port Facilities
You can enter the marina even at night time.

Electricity and water are available in the marina and in the yard. The depth of the sea in the marina is 15 feet and 270 yachts can be moored here. The yard can park up to 150 boats.

A fueling station, first aid, three bars and three restaurants, a private swimming sea platform, ship chandlery and laundry, are all services offered by the marina.

One supermarket is in the marina and two more are near the entrance.

The local market, held twice weekly in the city center, on Wednesdays and Saturdays, has fresh and very tasty seasonal vegetables and fruits and is only a five minute walk from the marina. Be sure not to miss tasting the oranges and other citrus fruits grown in Finike.

Near the marina there are some excellent restaurants. My favorite is a spacious restaurant with a terrace that overlooks the parking area. Mustafà serves delicious grilled lambchops and French fries. The atmosphere is very nice and if you are a guest of the marina or the yard, they will give you ten percent off the total bill. [Bill = Esap in Turkish]

Setur Finike Marina: www.seturmarinas.com

TEKIROVA (36°31'N 30°34'E)
From Finike, you have thirty-five miles to sail before approaching the beautiful anchorage of Tekirova. This bay is exposed to the southerly winds, which in summer are very unusual in this area. The harbor was once an important commercial center.

High pine trees and brightly colored oleanders grow around the arched beach in front of the anchorage.

Approaching the bay, it is best to proceed cautiously in the center of the inner channel, as there are some big rocks lying below that line the sides of the beach.

The sandy and muddy seafloor provides a good hold.

The archaeological site that overlooks the bay, on the cliff, is definitely worth a visit. The entrance ticket costs three dollars. Don't forget to bring your camera.

A refreshing swim in the clean, fresh water of the stream that flows by the side of the beach can be a good alternative to swimming in the sea. The warmer sea water is green and cloudy but clean.

Behind the beach, less than a yard away, a small campground is tucked in among the trees. There you can buy fresh fruit and vegetables from a tiny grocery shop, or drink a cold beer at the campground bar, where you can meet many friendly people.

KEMER MARINA (36°36'.2N 30°34'.3E)

Since 1984 when the marina first opened, it has aimed to present itself as the most important and busiest meeting place for sailors worldwide.

Thanks to its strategic position, between Europe and the Red Sea, a clever and enthusiastic management, its mild climate and perfect protection from sea storms, the Kemer Marina is indeed crowded all year round, especially when a large part of the sailing community spends their winters onboard their boats, using them like houses.

During the three- or four-month winter season, sailors, with the support of the marina office, organize bus tours around Turkey, language lessons, English traditional tea breaks onboard, cooking courses (with great interest in Italian cuisine, especially pasta), lessons on the maintenance and service of engines, and many more opportunities for exchange of information among the people staying there.

The atmosphere that reigns in the marina is one of friendliness and availability. If you intend to leave your boat for the winter season at the Kemer Marina it is best to contact them ahead of time and reserve by calling or writing to: Kemer Turkiz

Turban Marina 07980 Kemer, Antalya, tel. 0090 242 814 1490, fax 0090 242 814 1552, www.kemermarina.com

ANTALYA SETUR MARINA (36°50'.6N 30°37'E)

Usually, if you arrive in Antalya in the early afternoon, a breeze drives the boat on and, a gift from nature, it makes for fine sailing, with sea spray and the wind at your back.

Sailboats will have a hard time anchoring inside the small, old port of Antalya because the few places reserved for private boats are always occupied.

Many local gullets offering daily trips occupy ninety percent of the old port.

In the morning, when many of the gullets leave the port and when they return in the evening, their high speed makes a lot of noise and can wake you up.

At night, the proximity of the disco spoils the splendid back-drop of the port with the very loud non-stop rhythm of its overpowering music.

Therefore it is much better to anchor at Setur Antalya Marina (www.seturmarinas.com), which is in the commercial port about five miles southwest of town.

This new and elegant marina holds up to a hundred boats and is equipped with two travel lifts—60 and 200 tons.

Here, too, before entering, it is best to contact the marina office via VHF on Channel 9 and they will give you a berth.

Unfortunately, the town of Antalya can only be reached by bus or taxi.

Port Facilities

Each berth has water and electricity. A big travel lift can lift boats up to 50 tons. Many artisans do all sorts of work and can assist in case of electrical or engine problems.

There are a couple of well-stocked shops with spare parts and accessories for boats, a laundromat service and some excellent restaurants.

There is also a good supermarket and very clean lavatories.

Be sure not to miss

Go and walk to the old town where affordably priced carpets and kilims, copper and leather goods are on sale.

Try the drink made of a mix of water and a special yogurt called "Ayran." It has a distinct flavor that comes from its fermented milk ingredient, like a yogurt drink but with salt and no fruit flavoring. In the summer it is a very popular drink since it is an excellent thirst-quencher. You can enjoy it seated in one of the many cafés that overlook the old harbor from above.

If you have time, see the ancient city of Perge near Antalya (ten miles), or the amphitheater of Aspendos (approximately 35 miles east of Antalya), the best preserved theater of antiquity that seated up to 15,000 people.

GENERAL INFORMATION

Ideal for

In summertime, cruising in this area isn't dangerous, as the meltemi from Kalkan to Antalya is weak and slowly disappears when sailing eastbound. Light breezes and calm sea conditions are predominant in July and August.

In winter, however, terrible weather conditions with strong southerly gales make it difficult to navigate along the coast.

If you plan to cruise in November and May, check the weather forecast.

The cruises suggested in the previous pages provide sailing information suited to those who love to alternate navigations with excursions, especially sightseeing of archaeological sites. Some of the inland trips include visiting the country's natural richness as in the case of the gorges of Saklikent.

Wonderful days anchored in lovely coves can be alternated with efficient stops at modern marinas.

For this reason, the crew must be an expert crew and cautious during winter navigation. Less expertise but physical activity prevails in the summer season.

Weather

From the end of November to the middle of May, the weather can change quickly and gales can come from any direction, most frequently from the south.

During the summer season, the meltemi blows in the expanse of sea between Fethiye and Kas. From Kas the wind can be lighter and variable, but the breeze and winds come mostly from the west and follow the coastline.

In summertime thunderstorms are rare, but starting at the end of August there is a good chance of encountering quick storms.

Reference Pilot Books

While sailing in this area, we consulted *Turkish Waters and Cyprus Pilot*, by Rod Heikell, published by Imray.

Navigation Rules

Along this coast there are no forbidden navigation zones.

However, international navigation rules must be followed at all times, and the cruising permit called "transit log" must be obtained from any port of entry. It expires after one year. The visa on the passport expires after three months.

Connections

The Dalaman International Airport is closest to the harbor of Göcek (20 miles, and 40 dollars), and to the harbor of Fethiye (40 miles and 80 dollars). The distance is greater from Dalaman Airport to Kas (100 miles and 150 dollars) and Antalya (170 miles and 200 dollars).

The Antalya International Airport is less than ten miles from the city of Antalya. The distance from the airport of Antalya to Kemer is 35 miles and the price by taxi is 90 dollars.

Finike Marina is 70 miles from the airport of Antalya and the price is 120 dollars.

Distances

Fethiye – Kalkan:	40 miles
Kalkan – Kas:	10 miles
Kas – Kekova:	14 miles
Kekova – Finike:	22 miles
Finike – Tekirova:	35 miles
Tekirova – Kemer:	6 miles
Kemer – Antalya:	18 miles

Web Sites

Antalya International Airport: www.aytport.com
www.antalyamarina.com
www.allaboutturkey.com/antalya.htm
www.kemerturkizmarina.com
www.seturmarinas.com

PART 4

The Ionian Coast: From Izmir to Bodrum

Sigacik

With a strong wind astern, it didn't take long to sail to the town of Sigacik, so Nicoletta and I were busy furling the sail at the bow.

During our navigation we had consulted the nautical chart of the area and had decided that we would moor opposite the archaeological site of the ancient city of Teos, once home to a Greek port.

Seen from the chart, the anchorage seemed wonderful. It was supposed to be a well-protected bay, with a good seafloor depth of fifteen feet that is ideal for dropping anchor, and situated right in front of an interesting archaeological site, with a backdrop of hills, dotted with olive trees, that descend toward the sea.

Cape Killik is close by. We immediately recognized the

anonymous white buildings of a tourist village that stretched along a vast portion of the hilly terrain.

The dark gentle rocky slopes that extend from the cape to the site and gradually decline toward the sea are full of new construction, totally spoiling the magnificent setting of this ancient settlement, which, in the past, boasted a beautiful theater that towered over the hills.

Greenish murky water made it difficult for Nicoletta, who was at the bow, to see the seafloor properly, but she did notice that some areas, in the middle of the bay, had dangerous rocks protruding a few inches below sea level.

With her arm, she signaled to slow down even more, so I passed to neutral, and let the boat move simply by headway.

By advancing extremely slowly, we immediately perceived that the bay had a really annoying undertow.

"I don't like it," said Nicoletta worriedly as she came toward the cockpit, "First of all, I didn't expect to find all these semi-detached houses that mar the surrounding hills, and then this terrible undertow! It will have us rocking all night. We would be better off looking for a different anchorage," she suggested.

"I agree with you. Green water isn't appealing to swim in," and, irritated, I added, "how could they let them build hundreds of closely packed homes near an archaeological site like this one? They must be mad," I concluded. I turned the wheel, changed our route, and proceeded three miles north, to the little port of Sigacik, an undoubtedly more comfortable anchorage, it turned out.

The village of Sigacik was a stronghold. When seen from afar, the sight was so beautiful that it put us again in a good mood.

The bay at the entrance of the port was well protected. That night, we were assured of quiet water; thus, we'd be comfortable on board.

We dropped anchor north of the port entrance, not far from the muddy shallows that extend eastward.

The water here, too, was not crystal clear, but since it was nonetheless clean, we plunged in before our evening shower.

Though it was late afternoon, the sun beamed down on our wet bodies, and made us seek the shade of the canvas.

For centuries, the solid low stone walls of the fort have enclosed the village, which sits on flat land, facing the sea.

Jutting out from the reddish roof tiles, a white minaret glittered, reflecting the sun's rays.

I didn't see any boats moving in or out of port, not even in the bay where we were anchored.

The large bay, in fact, hosted only JANCRIS and one other sailboat, which was flying the German flag. West of us, a motor yacht was moored near the rocks, with two lines securing its stern to land.

"What about touring the land before dinnertime?" proposed Nicoletta.

"I'll get the dinghy ready while you get dressed," I replied and got up, my body already totally dry.

A few hundred feet away there was a short cement sea wall protected by enormous gray blocks.

I slowed down to enter the port, which was bigger than it had appeared on the chart. Its west side was dredged, and the land was bordered with cement blocks that formed a long dock, about six hundred feet long. In front, there were a couple of restaurants and a small road that led to the site of Teos.

A man came out of one of the two restaurants. He walked straight to the new dock to greet us, waving, and, in a loud voice, inquiring in English why we didn't come into port with our boat, showing us there was room.

I steered the dinghy, which was about a foot and a half above the seafloor, up to the dock and answered that we preferred anchoring our boat, since in the mornings we really like to go for a dip.

He smiled and nodded. Before leaving, we asked whether our dinghy could be left tied to the dock. We discovered that, though the shoal was dredged twelve feet, and therefore there would be no problem, it was still not allowed. He then walked away saying, "next year, God willing."

So with the engine back into gear, I accelerated with the bow pointing eastward, where a number of foreign boats and some caiques floated.

We decided that it would be best to leave our tender in the eastern part of the port, where the fortified citadel stands.

Among the boats moored there, we spotted a vessel flying an Italian flag, so we approached it.

Sigacik, the village minaret

The topsides had two large lines running across: a light blue one and a darker blue one. The prow had a big Phoenician eye, similar to the ones that are painted on the bows of Sicilian fishermen's boats. According to the seafaring tradition, the eye is a good luck charm that protects the vessel and its crew from the many dangers presented by the sea.

Between the two boats, the Italian one and its neighbor, roughly six feet away, there was enough room for us to moor our dinghy and tie it to the dock.

The Italian boat did not seem to have anyone onboard, as there was no noise or movement coming from within.

"They must somewhere around here, visiting the area, like we want to do" said Nicoletta, taking my hand and pulling me away from the boat.

Though the new concrete dock was still not finished, it seemed to be well built. In the future, energy and water will also be supplied.

Just behind, the marshy area there faded away as we approached the village.

Then, in large block letters the word BAZAAR crowned a large white arch.

Next to the arch, on what seemed an abandoned patch of grass, we spotted a strange white stone sculpture in the shape of a heart, which stood over three feet tall.

"A strange village," said Nicoletta as she stroked the sculpture.

We climbed a few steps, walked under an arch, and found ourselves in the bazaar.

Not many people were there but the few who were seemed cheerful and greeted us kindly.

The stalls sold some cheap-looking handicrafts; even the shop windows were not particularly appealing.

Proceeding on our tour, we ended in a small covered area, probably the fruit market, but due to our timing, very few fruits or vegetables were left.

When finally out and in the sun-drenched road, we realized that we were in a dirt lot, probably a parking area.

Just a little further ahead, we saw large fortress walls and a couple of tall, thin palm trees with emerald green crowns standing at the sides of the gate marking its position.

Inside the fortress, a spiral staircase with stone steps led to the top of the square tower, and at the same time offered some shade. We made our way up, and just as our eyes were getting accustomed to the darkness of the staircase, we approached the top, which at some point started reeking of urine and mold. We had to hold our breath and climb the last slippery stone steps as fast as we could.

Once we were out, a fresh sea breeze filled the air, and we could finally behold the splendid view from above.

Magically positioned, the sun radiated in the sky and tinged in amber all it touched.

From the top of the tower we could see JANCRIS, immobile, on the calm seawater of the bay, its two aluminium masts, at times struck by sun beams, emitting a glitter of warm light.

The German boat, not far from JANCRIS, had its dinghy tied to stern, indicating that people were onboard. From the motor yacht, a big tender sped away, leaving a long white slipstream behind.

Turning our backs to the sea, we saw the terracotta red rooftops of houses where they emerged from the fortress, dotting the verdant inner courtyards with color.

Some of the roofs were round in shape, typically Arab in style, and a small white mosque with its tall, thin minaret rose in the center of the village. Above the cupola, its rooftop, a metallic crescent moon shone, reflecting the fiery rays of the setting sun.

"You go down first," said Nicoletta, pushing me toward the staircase, "otherwise, with you behind me, forcing me to rush down, I risk falling on these smooth, steep steps.

And with such a stench, I would hate having my butt on the ground."

I led the way and headed down the narrow staircase. She followed, but being very careful about where she put her feet, it took her longer to get down. "All this time waiting for you . . . I thought you had fallen," I said ironically. She, on the other hand, came happily up to me, rushing to be out in the open air.

"I went slowly," she said taking my hand, and added "do you feel like pasta and tuna, for two, on board? I am so hungry."

"Sounds good," I answered, "but let's go through with the end of the tour and reach the dinghy by taking the little village streets we saw from above. They looked so charming."

The route meandered along streets with old stone houses and new pastel colored ones where children played, and as we passed them they interrupted their games to smile and say "Hallo, hallo!"

Sitting in front of their houses, some elderly women, wearing scarves around their heads, would raise their eyes to look at us, smile, and nod.

As we walked around, men, young women, and everyone in general, smiled and greeted us. Since they acknowledged our presence with such kindness and gentleness, we felt happy and more at ease.

Out of the blue, from the garden of a lovely stone house, we heard someone speak Italian.

The garden, with its well-manicured lawn, its trees, and its large, pink stone-paved walkway was enclosed by a wrought iron fence.

The villa, in its style and flair, seemed Italian. From the beautiful wooden front gate came the unmistakable voice of a man who, walking next to a woman, went into the garden.

"Buona sera," I said as we passed by his house.

"Buona sera," replied the man with the moustache and immediately asked, "Are you Italian?"

"Of course. And so are you, it would seem," I replied.

"Right. What a coincidence, since there aren't many Italians here," he said cheerfully, moving closer to the gate and adding, "You must be the owners of the beautiful sailboat I noticed while I was driving here."

"Yes, it is ours. And this beautiful, old, but newly restored house must be yours."

"Indeed, it is," he replied, and drew the brunette standing next to him even closer. He added, "My wife is an architect. I bought the run-down property very cheaply, and she restored it. Originally, this house was an old Turkish public bath, which deteriorated over the years. Now, the house has many rooms," he concluded proudly.

"Would you like to see it?" asked the wife, looking at Nicoletta.

"I sure would," she answered with a big smile.

The interior had a vault ceiling, blending ochre colored walls with stone walls, creating a cozy and elegant atmosphere. The floor was paved mostly in stone but some rooms, as in the kitchen, had terracotta tiles.

"We are still not living in the house but expect to move in soon," said Alberto, the owner.

Chatting with our new friends made time fly, and as dinnertime soon approached, they proposed we dine out, in one of the restaurants by the sea, where the food is good and the prices are too.

A quick exchange of glances between Nicoletta and I confirmed immediately that we would accept the invitation.

We all walked toward the harbor where the restaurants were and our dinghy was waiting for us.

Small tables, all lit by candlelight, were hidden under trees; nearby, a low building accomodated a kitchen and a large grill. That night, the restaurateur, apparently a friend of Alberto's, advised us to try the grilled stone bass and that is what we ended up having.

At dinner we mentioned that we had seen another sailboat flying the Italian flag, but no one seemed to be on board.

Alberto looked at his wife and said happily, "I told you that very soon this place would have greater tourism. It is an important thing to finish the harbor quickly," he concluded looking at me.

"You are right," I replied, and suddenly a voice from behind us butted in.

"I totally agree," said a tanned man in his fifties with short salt-and-pepper hair. He cheerfully added, "Sorry to barge in, but as I was walking past, I just happened to hear you speak Italian so I could not help but interrupt you. It is so rare to see Italians here in Turkey. My wife and I have been sailing for a couple of months along this coast and we have only come across one other Italian boat. But there are plenty of Germans and English in this area."

"Have you already had dinner?" asked Alberto.

"To tell you the truth, we wanted to eat at this restaurant," he replied with a slight sense of embarrassment.

Alberto, raising his hand, called the waiters, who immediately did their best. In no time, another table and two chairs were added to ours.

After the usual, customary introductions, we all had many stories and anecdotes to share. We were three couples who had never met before, seated around a table enjoying their evening, and being totally ourselves, without having to impress the others.

The following day, each couple would proceed along their course, taking with them the lightheartedness of our conversations, without any unspoken ends or motives. Unfortunately, our beautiful and musical Italian language is not very common in far away places around the world, so we are often obliged to speak a foreign language, usually English, which, though we can speak it, entails some effort.

That evening, seated at the table, I felt I was amid true friends. It felt like years ago, in the summer, when good old school friends and I met at a restaurant out on the Euganean hills, near our city of Padua, to eat under a verdant pergola and escape the city's summer heat.

Well, that evening, in an unknown Turkish village, in the company of compatriots, I felt that same sensation—I smiled and laughed in the same way, and was as happy as you are when you know that you are in the right company. I was there for the pure pleasure of being with other people, to speak and listen to our beautiful Italian language.

The Storm

With the jib eased so as to have as much wind as possible, we glided quickly toward our destination. At times, the jib's white cloth hid the rocky profile of the desert islet of Cavus that unmistakably marks the entry of the bay where we were headed.

On top of the hill, where the meltemi blows, sits a military observation tower. The hill is nothing but a promontory that protects the bay and the village of Gumusluk from the open sea.

When you approach from the north, the entrance of the bay appears only at the very last minute; when navigating, our course had pointed to the islet of Cavus. We had reached our destination in just the amount of time we had scheduled the evening before.

Nicoletta lowered the mizzen sail while I rolled the jib and hauled the sheet in tightly.

It took only a few minutes for JANCRIS to lower its sails and be propelled by its solid and reliable engine. We moved along the narrow channel and found that the water inside the bay was calm.

Upon entering, the first thing that struck us were the ruins of the picturesque defense tower built on the rocks of the islet of Tavsan, south of the bay. In ancient days, it must have served to block and prevent the entry of enemy ships.

Many boats were anchored: there were several caiques, but also plenty of sailboats, and even a couple of small motor yachts.

As we proceeded slowly northward, in the direction of a golden sand beach, Nicoletta, from the bow, had found the right spot to drop the anchor.

There were gusts of wind, at times blowing over twenty-five knots, which lifted eddies of dust on the beach that would disperse at sea.

When about thirty feet from the shore, I got into reverse gear and dropped the anchor. It rattled its way toward the seafloor and planted itself so as to tame the bow, so that it would set itself windward.

Nicoletta made her way from the bow to the well-protected cockpit, which always provides great shelter from the wind thanks to its fiberglass top.

"It looks like a good anchorage," she said, as I turned the engine off. Then, running her fingers through her hair, which the wind had ruffled up, she added, "And it also looks as if the meltemi does not seem inclined to blow any less intensely; on the contrary, it seems to be picking up more and more violently."

"Indeed. It's still a very stiff wind," I answered. "Let's hope it drops after sunset, as it normally does," I concluded, perceiving the sceptical look on her face.

Being rather narrow, the bay is well protected from the waves of the sea, so the boat swayed from the wind but did not roll from the waves.

We decided that after lunch we would disembark and go for a walk, looking westward to see the condition of the open sea.

To reach the beach we lowered our tender. Once there we lifted it out of the water and placed its keel on the large-grained sand.

The few trees that fringe the beach were swaying as though they were being slapped by the sudden gusts of wind that came swooping down from the bare rocky promontory. Large greenish patches of Mediterranean vegetation adorned the white stones of the hill.

We took a tiny path that climbs up to the promontory toward the open sea. Behind us, we left the low stone houses that are set just behind the beach, and which we had not noticed from the boat since they were hidden by the trees. Basically the houses were found only around the beach, leaving the western part at the base of the promontory deserted.

We walked making sure we avoided the many thorny plants that grow there—they would surely have scratched our legs and made us bleed.

Now and again we stopped to lift our gaze to the distance and admire the panorama that unfolded before our eyes.

The howling wind made the steel shrouds of the sailboats anchored in the bay tinkle, creating music that echoed in our ears. Undoubtedly a little worried, we nonetheless stopped to watch the boats dance with every gust that came along.

The show was beautiful and fascinated us even though one of the protagonists of the dance was JANCRIS. Even from afar, we always recognized her because of her callipygian shape.

The path, midway across the hill, led toward the open sea. From there, we could enjoy what seemed like a boundless view.

When we returned home from the around-the-world tour, after navigating for two years, our time was spent watching the horizon and beyond, hoping we would be the first to spot an island emerging from the blue seawater so that we could land on it. But when we were back in the city, we realized that the horizon there is limited, interrupted and hidden by buildings and other barriers built by man.

The feeling is disheartening, and for a time it seemed to have taken me over, trapping me, and confining me between the boundaries of the walls of my home and those of the city I lived in. I could not imagine, just over the horizon, what an extraordinary island I would go on to discover and what remarkable people I would meet.

Before seeing its dark profile in the distance, you can smell the island. It is the scent of the land and its inhabitants who have absorbed the flavor of the food provided by Mother Nature.

The mountainous profile of the Greek islands of Kalimnos and Leros could be seen in the distance; further south, the islet of Pserimos was clearly distinguishable by its cone-shaped hill.

The deep blue, crisp, clear sky was of color typical of the Aegean area—one that has been swept clean by the meltemi wind, which blows intensely in this entire area, probably from the Cyclades to the Sporades islands, and then south from Rhodes to Crete.

Without recognizing the boundaries that man has traced, the eye extends to the Turkish coast where we are now—including the gulf of Bodrum and Marmaris.

The sea below crashed against the rocks and turned into a snow white foam.

As far as the eye could see, the deep blue seawater was dotted with the white crests of waves that, thanks to a play of light and shade, seemed like long gentle hills of water which, as they move south, become increasingly mighty and devastating.

Though enchanted by the show nature had put on, I predicted that a storm was on its way.

Nicoletta's gaze crossed mine. Though she was worried about what the weather had in store, the idea that JANCRIS was anchored in a bay that was protected from terrible waves in a storm comforted us both somewhat.

"We are lucky to be in a bay with this kind of weather," said Nicoletta smiling. "We are not moving from here until the storm has passed," she added categorically, and turned to look at the calm green water where we had anchored.

"Don't worry," I answered, "we are in no hurry . . . the world tour is over. Back then, because it was a regatta with scheduled dates, we had to set off and sail in all kinds of weather all the time, even when there was a low pressure. Do you remember how terrible it was to sail from the island of Madeira to the Canary Islands? How sick we were, and how many bucketfuls of water got poured on us on for what seemed like endless days?"

"I sure do remember," she answered with a slight grimace on her tanned face, "For that reason, and if at all possible, I would like to avoid that kind of sailing, which was really no fun. It often makes you ask yourself what you are doing it all for. Fortunately, in this case, the winds are arriving in tandem with the sun and a blue sky. Just think how desolate it would be if they came with the rain and a storm!" she concluded, her grimace giving way to a cheerful smile.

On the way back, we decided to make a short detour along the narrow entry of the bay, where, on the opposite side, stood the ruins of the ancient defense tower.

Closer to the water, big smooth pebbles gave way to shingles that became finer and finer and eventually turned to sand on the shore.

Once we had reached the entry channel, from closer up, we could see the ruins of the small stone tower, which today had boisterous kids using it as a diving platform.

My curiosity was drawn to a few square-shaped, semi-submerged rocks that were a few steps away from me.

They could have been the foundation of a building, perhaps a tower that has now disappeared, and which was paired to another tower in front of me.

Then, observing it with a little more attention, I discarded the idea of a twin construction because the square stones cover a vaster area that extends some feet along the beach.

From the rocky cliff I was on, I leaped to the ground, on the shingles, and walked over the stones to try and discover the shape of its walls.

Nicoletta, who remained atop of the rocky cliff, watched me. Smiling, she must have been asking herself what on earth I was doing.

"Come down," I said to her, accompanying the words with a hand gesture. "Look what I found," I insisted in a triumphant voice.

Not certain whether to go along with the joke, or if perhaps it wasn't a joke, she jumped on the beach and, unsure, moved up to me without ever abandoning the smirk she had on her face. "Trust me," I said, "I am not fooling you. Hurry up, look and you'll be surprised!" I concluded, as I moved the shingles with my foot, but a few steps away from the sea.

In doing so I unveiled a small part of an ancient red and pink mosaic floor that had been buried underneath.

The smile she had on her face disappeared and her jaw dropped in amazement. Without uttering a single word, Nicoletta crouched to admire the small patch of mosaic floor. She moved the pebbles away gently to expand the exposed surface area.

Looking around her, with a furtive air, as though she had found a treasure, she got up, and standing there whispered to me as if she had made an exciting discovery that must not be revealed to others, especially to local authorities.

"You think that the Turkish authorities don't know that there is a mosaic floor down here?" I asked her, laughing. Then, without even waiting for her answer, I added, "they know everything, even how many little pieces of mosaic are down here. They are the ones who hide them beneath the sand. They do this because they don't have any funds for their excavation and, by keeping them buried and thus hidden, they can preserve them. So tell me what you think was built here—a Byzantine church or a Roman villa?"

"I think it is the floor of a Byzantine church" she replied, laughing, but then with enthusiasm, she said: "In any case I feel that I am a part of a wonderful discovery. To me, it is as if we were the ones who uncovered this ancient find. Can you imagine that centuries ago people walked on it? Who can tell what this place was really like in those days. Now it is only a fishermen's village of some thirty homes and a road that disappears into the sea. Turkey is unique!" she concluded and crouched over once again, this time to cover the colored mosaic.

"Let's go back to the boat," I proposed, grabbing her hand to help her up.

The wind was blowing more fiercely as sunset approached.

The boat had stayed where it was; the anchor did not drag, perhaps thanks to the two hundred feet of chain we had dropped.

Sitting under the fiberglass top, protected from the wind, I looked at the other boats anchored near us and noted that a 40-foot motorboat had slightly moved from its original position. Its tall fly design, which lets the captain steer from the top deck, created resistance against the wind and hence the anchor did not hold its ground against the strong gusts of wind.

The man on board had realized it too and was nervously walking fore and aft to check the situation with the chain.

"I believe the boat next to us is having some problems with their mooring," I said to Nicoletta who had come up to the cockpit in order to check out what was happening.

"They don't want to re-anchor but know very well that the anchor won't hold the way it is now. And if this weren't enough, they are also aware that in less than an hour it will be dark. Not a good situation," I concluded.

Then suddenly, I saw the motor yacht's engine exhaust pipes fume black smoke, a sign that he wanted to moor again.

"Great idea," said Nicoletta.

A dark-haired woman, with her head down trying to protect herself from the gusts of the wind, headed toward the bow to lift the anchor by using the windlass control.

Not a simple maneuver because the violent wind swayed the boat right and left as if it were a cork.

At times the water whipped bucketfuls of water on deck and onto the woman standing at the bow. At times, we heard her cry out sharply as she recovered the anchor chain slowly and with great effort. All of a sudden, the man at the wheel, to counter a gust of wind that would move his boat too close to JANCRIS, abruptly accelerated to move away from us and windward, nearer to the coast.

Just as all this was taking place, I spotted a buoy, the same buoy I had seen during our walk on land.

For a second a thought flashed in my head and I realized that the motor yacht could be secured to that buoy. All that was needed was to ease about thirty feet of chain. This would allow the boat to go back far enough and be closer to the buoy, which would then be tied with a mooring line.

Once in place, the anchor and the buoy together would surely hold, even under strenuous conditions.

"Right!" I said, dashing to join Nicoletta astern knowing that she had not yet picked up on my intentions.

Before climbing onto the dinghy I filled her in on my plan and then quickly set off toward the other boat.

The man, seeing me approach, moved away from the control station and leaned out to the side.

I moved closer and in English told him how I thought we could proceed.

He saw the buoy and with a big smile of gratitude nodded and lifted his thumb.

He moved closer to his wife to explain the new maneuver. She suddenly seemed to understand and appreciate my suggestion since I saw her look at me and then wave with gestures of thanks.

Little by little, the chain was eased and the boat backed slowly, closer to the buoy.

Then, out of the blue, the woman at the bow became agitated about something. She had called the man and he seemed to have understood the problem.

They have no more chain, I thought to myself.

In fact the captain rushed to the aft locker to get a long line. He fell, but eventually he managed and sprang back to the bow where he fumbled a while with the mooring line and finally succeeded in lowering the last bit of chain and then tying the line, which was blocked on a bitt, so that it could be controlled.

I went toward the buoy, held fast onto it, and waited for the boat to backtrack closer. I watched the entire maneuver, sopping wet and chilled, as I held with all of my strength onto the buoy, while my tender reared at every wave.

The sun had by now disappeared behind the promontory but the wind did not stop whipping up the water in the bay, lifting clouds of vaporized seawater that at times prevented me from keeping my eyes open or even from breathing.

I finally saw the white topside of the boat draw nearer to me. From one of the lockers astern, I saw the woman extract a long, sturdy mooring line, while from the bow, the man was skilfully easing the line that was tied to the chain.

The woman, before swinging the line to me, was carefully calculating her throw in my direction but then began shaking her head.

In fact, we were too far away and with such wind the line would never reach me.

I let go of the buoy and sped toward their boat. Once there, I grabbed onto the side and had her pass me the whole coiled mooring line.

We had no time to waste, as even if the man had blocked the boat, at every gust of wind, it kept distancing itself from the buoy.

I darted back to the buoy steering the dinghy blindly, for my eyes burned and I was frozen.

I lifted the white floating ball that had a big ring around which you fasten the line and passed the line I had carried aboard through the ring. In a flash, it was tied with a thumb knot.

I then turned and looked in the direction of the motor yacht.

It was about thirty feet from me.

Good! I thought that the mooring line was twice that length so what mattered now was to make sure that no knots or coils appear, since this would mean trouble.

I got into reverse gear, and with one foot I held down the other end of the line.

The line glided smoothly out of the tender, creating no problems. Every now and then, I made sure that I turned to see the boat with the man at the bow anxiously waiting.

I reached him, and then I stood up and passed him the other end of the line.

He grabbed it with such force that I understood just how anxiously he had been waiting for this moment. He immediately secured it to the free bitt.

Then he also recovered the line tied to the chain and hauled it in as tight as possible.

Holding our breath, we stood there for a while, our muscles very tense, waiting.

A gust came, then another, and an even more violent gust.

We looked carefully, trying to figure out if the boat had changed its position with such a wind. But no, the buoy and anchor seem to have managed to oppose the strength of the wind successfully.

The dark-haired woman came to the bow, she put her arm around the man's hips, and looked more relaxed. She smiled showing gratitude; he too smiled happily and invited me on board.

I thanked them for the invitation but I could not wait to re-turn back to JANCRIS, as I felt colder and colder and all I wanted was to take a beautiful warm shower, and stay away from the wind.

Nicoletta waited for me astern, ready to take the line and tie the dinghy. She seemed to be proud of me and was happy for them.

As I set foot on JANCRIS I got rid of my soaking shirt and drenched pants. Dripping and chilled to the bone, I de-scended from the cockpit indoors to enjoy a nice hot shower.

When I finally reappeared, I saw Nicoletta smile as she handed me a glass of white wine. I took it and sat on the bench to sip and savor it.

"All seems under control onboard the motorboat," com-mented Nicoletta, looking at the indoor lights that ap-peared from the motor yacht.

"They were lucky to have been near a buoy; otherwise I don't think their anchor would have stayed in place, not in this kind of wind, even if they repeated the anchoring maneuver," I answered. With an ironic smile, I added, "Just imagine that on a boat like that one they only have a hundred and fifty feet of chain. It's way too short because when there is lots of strong wind, all the force is concen-trated on the anchor, without being absorbed by the chain lying on the seafloor," I concluded shaking my head.

"I wouldn't be so surprised," she interjected. "Remember the first year we sailed—how many nights we spent awake checking the anchors since the size of the anchor was too small for our boat, and we too had too little chain? These mistakes come from a lack of experience, by those who have spent their nights in safe harbors or marinas, and not in bays. In any case, they were not only lucky to have the buoy, but they were also fortunate to have had you," she concluded as she leaned toward me and kissed me.

Sea Gypsies

No guide ever mentions the sea gypsies, nor do chart books say anything of their presence; even the most complete guides do not provide information about these people. Yet they exist, and all along the jagged Turkish coast there are more and more of them.

It must be stressed that these gypsies are not the ones that you see in European cities; the ones here do not live by begging.

Their life is a nomads' life but aboard a small, poor wooden boat. Some may resemble the gullets that are typical of this Mediterranean area, though they are often more elongated and narrower.

The vessels generally have a noisy inboard engine that propels the craft slowly, going at about six knots, from bay to bay.

With a strong meltemi astern, I have seen the people on some of these boats hoist wood masts and climb up to mount a small sail in order to switch the engine off and save precious fuel.

In the bays we visited, and where sea gypsies are known to live, I have seen families living on board with as many as eight members. When they move, they usually do so in small groups, of two or three boats.

One of the many picturesque inlets along the coast, with the
boats of the sea gypsies

To survive, they fish, and, in the summer season, more
and more of them frequent the tourist-rich bays in order to
offer their catch of fish either to the restaurants or to the
boats anchored there.

Some of the gypsies I have come across are very re-
sourceful, and I have seen them send their sisters or wives
on board a small rowboat to sell handcrafted products to
the boats spending their time in the bay.

The women dress in a very simple way, with a veil covering their hair even on the hottest summer days, and their
kindness and patience make them extremely able vendors.

As far as I know and have heard about these gypsies,
no illegal or violent conduct, including theft, can be attrib-
uted to them. They are honest people, and they live according to their ancient tradition; they are free-spirited
and do not have any bonds with the populations of inland
villages.

They tend to moor some feet from the shore, dropping

an anchor astern, while the bow is firmly secured by tying a line around a tree or a rock outcropping. When no trees or rocks can be used, another system to secure their prow is to drop a grapnel anchor near the shore so it easily grips the rocky bottom.

In the evenings, especially in bays that are less populated, they sit on the beach, around a fire, and without ever disturbing the peace of the other boats in the bay, they eat and chat around the fire.

Women sea gypsies usually sleep on board, on mats that are covered with carpets, while the men sleep in hammocks that hang wherever they think is most suited. In the morning, if they decide to move on, they set sail very early. What is remarkable, though, is that they leave no traces of their presence on the beach, not so much as a piece of paper.

On board, placed somewhere in the center, sit old ice cream refrigerators, the ones that look like containers and open from the top. Obviously the compressors don't work, but it doesn't matter since they use it as an icebox, to deposit, at the bottom, big frozen ice blocks that they find in ports and in coastal villages.

Their sense of orderliness and aesthetics leads them to paint their refrigerators the same color as the hull, preferring colors like red or light blue.

Another accessory that is never missing aboard their boats is a canvas cover. They mount it on the boat's iron frame so that it seems almost permanent, and it generally covers about two thirds of the boat.

Sea gypsies are always very kind to seafarers, and when JANCRIS crossed their route, they waved at us enthusiastically.

On several occasions, our boat was the only foreign craft anchored in a bay where they had also decided to spend the night. This factor never worried or bothered us— quite the contrary—their presence represented a positive sign, since they have a profound knowledge of the coast, and this meant that the bay was extremely safe and well sheltered.

I recall that once, a long time ago, we had anchored JANCRIS in a deserted bay, whose surrounding low hills were not covered by houses—there were only white rocks and silvery olive trees.

The bay had no other boats moored there despite its picturesque, shallow, transparent waters. After having sailed all morning we were rather tired and didn't feel like lowering the tender into the water, even in view of the fact that we would be leaving the following morning, so as the beach was not very far off, and the water a tempting turquoise, we decided to swim to shore.

Nicoletta, who is great swimmer, challenged me to a race, but I was no match for her, so she got there first.

When I finally made it, I was prepared to endure her triumphant air as she joked and poked fun at me. Instead, her face showed an expression of worry that stemmed from the fact that she had just noticed that there were three boats of gypsies here we had not seen before. The boats were pulled ashore, and they had set up a camp base in the shade of some century-old olive trees close to the beach.

They must have been there for some time, probably at least several days, because they had unloaded quite a bit of material from the boats.

When we reached the beach, we sat on the dry sand to dry our skin in the sun. This was not the first time that we had shared a beach with sea gypsies, so we knew that there was no reason to worry; however, the feeling of being observed by the eyes of so many strangers made us uneasy, perhaps even because we were in bathing suits while they were, as their custom dictated, fully dressed, their bodies covered completely, especially the women.

It took us but a few minutes to decide that we would

leave and swim toward JANCRIS. A woman in the group, see-ing that we were about to leave the beach, came up to us. She was young, with a kind looking face, two big black slightly almond shaped eyes, her long coal black hair braided, reaching her back.

Despite her loose, dark colored pants and the couple of shirts she wore under her light colored flower-patterned blouse, you could see she had a stout and solid body build, like most Turkish women. Maybe it is the hard and exhausting jobs they do.

She knew very little English, but we understood that she was inviting us to tea. Nicoletta looked at me a little per-plexed, she didn't want to accept the invitation, but at the same time did not want to offend the young woman, so with a wide smile she nodded.

When the girl understood that we had accepted, a big smile appeared on her beautiful face, revealing a set of perfect white teeth.

We followed her along the sandy path that led us to the campsite. There, a little pot of water was boiling over the burning flame of the fire.

Children, three or four of them, came to greet us, laugh-ing, while the adults who had been squatting got up, waved, and pointed their hands toward the ground, that is the sand, to get us to sit, so we did just that.

Nicoletta in her bikini felt rather uncomfortable, but didn't want to show it, and I smiled to everyone around to find that they smiled back.

These people, I figured, were probably three different generations of the same family: the grandparents, parents and children. The grandparents must have had three chil-dren who in turn married and had the children that were cheerfully playing on the sand next to us.

The three men, undoubtedly brothers, were more or less my age.

No one spoke comprehensible English, so after spending

a few seconds in a rather heavy silence, I broke the ice and stammered the few words I knew in Turkish.

My performance took them aback a little, and every word I uttered produced great laughter. Looking at each other amused, they even tried correcting my pronunciation.

They were extremely kind and endlessly repeated the sentence I had said until my consonants and accents were correct.

Despite the linguistic barriers, we managed to exchange a brief dialogue while sipping the strong, hot tea the Turks call "cay." The ordinary tea sold in the carpet shops just doesn't compare to the gypsies' cay.

From the conversation, we understood that one of the boats had engine problems. The next morning some of the men would leave and go to a nearby village by boat to search for the spare part. Once we finished our tea and our very limited linguistic repertoire of Turkish words, we thanked them sincerely and took the path that led to the sea.

Before we could leave, the woman who had come to call Nicoletta earlier wanted to give us a piece of goat cheese preserved in a yellowish liquid, in a plastic container. As she opened the red lid of the container, a sour, pungent smell of goat emanated, taking our breath away.

Nicoletta, who had understood the girl's intention, continued to smile charmingly, but launched an intense look my way, hoping that I would intervene and refuse the gift, which we did not appreciate but was so precious to them, without offending them.

On the spur of the moment I managed to invent that I have a terrible allergy to the cheese and therefore could not accept the gift.

Naturally to explain an allergy in a foreign language was no easy task, but with a little mime, I had the feeling that we had succeeded and they understood what I had said.

This conviction of mine was confirmed when I heard an

"Ah" come from the eldest brother's mouth who had explained to the others my problem and they, as a sign of respect, didn't laugh or joke.

And while I was at it, I added that since we truly appreciated their intent we would be happy to have a little of the wonderful tea.

Happy, the girl handed a paper bag to Nicoletta containing the aromatic leaves.

When we reached the shore, we once again turned back to wave goodbye.

They were all standing there, smiling, watching us move away. Nicoletta swam toward JANCRIS using only one hand as in the other she kept the tea leaves.

We spent the evening sitting astern, each holding a warm cup of the delightfully aromatic infusion, immersed in the pitch darkness; for quite a few minutes we remained there just looking in the direction of the beach where a flame shimmered.

"Just think," I said to Nicoletta, "that in these tormented years of the new millennium, there are still people living their way, according to tradition. How can their children integrate themselves in the western ways of living? You saw the way they laughed and played. . . . just happy to pick up sticks from the ground and invent a game, or from a shell they find lying on the sand, make up a fairy tale, since they have such imagination. At their age our friends' children spend time on Play Stations and computers. What astounds me is that Europe is just a few miles from here, and Turkey will sooner or later join Europe. What will happen to all these overly naive and "ignorant" people? How will they survive some of the rules imposed by Western society, which tends to trap people with prohibitions and rules, where if you don't adjust and follow, you are marginalized and made invisible until you finally disappear from the face of the earth?" I concluded, sipping that warm aromatic beverage.

GUIDE FROM IZMIR TO BODRUM

Izmir, Eskifoça, Ildir, Sigacik, Kusadasi, Saint Paul's Port, Asin, Yalikavak, Gumusluk, Bodrum

These destinations represent a different kind of cruises along the beautiful Turkish coast. They depart from the route the usual charter flotillas or gullets take. They allow you to discover places and anchorages as yet undiscovered by mass tourism, so try and get there before it is too late.

The route hugs an indented coastline and rewards any sailor with an opportunity to see some spectacular sea- and landscapes.

Many anchorages and tiny harbors are well protected from the predominant winds, have clean, turquoise water with only silver olive trees onshore, covering the landscape.

With the exception of the bigger harbors of Izmir and Bodrum, all the others are very picturesque, rather quiet, and never too busy. Here, time goes by slowly, with a different rhythm than in the city, the way nature intended.

In the little village that goes by the name of Sigacik, a simple way of life goes on pleasantly. With a lifestyle based on fishing, for generations the inhabitants have lived by a calm sea shaded by an enchanting Genovese fortress, as part and parcel of their normal existence. Very old olive trees cover the rocky ground with their tiny silver-green leaves, swaying in the summer wind.

Ancient ruins, long forgotten, are now hidden by vegetation or the sea. Walking ashore in this part of the Turkish coast, it is quite likely you will stumble upon some ancient handmade crafts. One day, Nicoletta and I were strolling along the Gumusluk beach, and beneath my feet, when I moved the sand, a small part of some ancient mosaic floor appeared. Who knows—it once may have formed part of a Byzantine church or an even older Roman villa. The stones and ruins of such buildings often

Archeological site of Bergama, a day excursion from Izmir

have been utilized to build the houses in the villages, as it is not unusual in the Mediterranean to see a mix of architectural styles. You might see churches built on Greek theater ruins, which before that were a mausoleum and maybe prior to that, celebrated some divinity.

Rent a car, or, even better, jump in a taxi, and go on an inland journey to visit some of the most famous archaeological sites. Don't miss the old theater of Bergama near Izmir, and Ephesus near Kusadasi.

In the following pages I will attempt to outline the best and most comfortable navigation course, providing winds and seas are favorable, leaving from the northern harbor of Izmir. You will be sailing in an area of the Aegean that is under rapid transformation. Unfortunately, many tour operators and building contractors are bringing new tourist villages and hotels to beautiful natural landscapes.

IZMIR (38°25'.4N 27°07'.6E OLD HARBOR POSITION)

This is the best place to change crew, thanks to its proximity to the international airport, and its good connections with Istanbul by ferry.

Izmir is the third biggest city in Turkey, where you can find whatever you need.

One legend has it that the famous ancient poet Homer was born in this city. Just over on the Greek island of Kios, however, the inhabitants there choose to tell a different story. In any case neither of them has come up with any definite proof.

When you sail into Izmir's old harbor you have to drop your anchor in a solid ground of thick, black mud, and berth stern-to, in its northeastern corner. Three-hundred feet of the public wharf is for yachts in transit, and I would suggest you stop in the harbor if you are planning on staying just overnight because the traffic of ferries and commercial ships make for rowdy companions. This is further exacerbated by the noise from the city going on behind the harbor. But although this anchorage is not idyllic, nearby, you have the advantages of numerous big supermarkets within easy walking distance, and an extensive big characteristic bazaar offering all sorts of products, from fresh fruit and vegetables to Turkish clothes and handicrafts.

If you intend to stay longer, it is better to go to the Levent Marina, a few miles southwest of the old harbor. Just remember to book in advance because space is very limited. Before entering the basin of the marina, you are well advised to contact the dock master by VHF on Channel 16 or 73. The marina is not very big, so if you have a 65-foot boat you have to watch how you berth.

Port Facilities

The marina's berthing capacity stands at 70 yachts, with electricity and water available for each berth as well as fuel dock, wireless Internet, hot showers, a 24-hour security watch, laundry services, and chandlery. The yard is near the marina and can accommodate 40 yachts, with a slipway that possesses a lift capacity of 250 tons. This marina and yard have a good reputation for wood and engine repairs and the big, well equipped carpenter shop will take on any job for you, as well as offering other services like painting and welding, lathe, sail and fiberglass repairs. The marina offers a good restaurant where you can eat European cuisine though prices are not cheap. You can find an affordable tavern close to the bazaar that serves typical regional cuisine. Fifteen minutes by taxi and you are in the center of Izmir. The marina office will help you to organize any inland journeys.

www.levent-marina.com

E-mail: tarik@levent-marina.com.tr

ESKI FOÇA (38°40'.2N 26°44'.7E)

I suggest an early departure from the deep Izmir Gulf before the wind picks up. Mile after mile, the noise of the city fades away and the color of the seawater is gradually restored to its clean and cobalt blue.

The small town of Eski Foça is surrounded by tiny islands, and on approaching you can do little other than admire the beauty of the coast, drop anchor, and indulge in a refreshing swim.

The best anchorage is a couple of miles north of the harbor, between Orak island and the mainland. A long, narrow sandbar located in this area bestows a turquoise color upon the sea. Drop the anchor in ten feet of water close to the sandbar, but if you plan to swim, watch out for the strong riptide.

If you intend on spending the night ashore you can drop the anchor in the well-protected water of the bay in front of the village of Eski Foça, and berth stern-to the dock in the best spot of the town. The depth is 25 feet and the muddy and sandy bottom makes an excellent holder. From the boat, you can see the slender minaret and powerful Genovese fortress just a few yards from the dock. Walking among the stalls with fresh fruit and vegetables on display, colored carpets and kilims, you can take in the friendly and peaceful atmosphere in what is a clean and tranquil village.

Along the promenade, some waterfront restaurants and cafés can appear a bit touristy, but the food is good and the prices reasonable. If you prefer real Turkish cuisine, you have to walk to the town center and try out the available taverns. Before you order, though, be advised to ask if they serve beer or wine, as in a typical Turkish tavern, you won't find any. Make sure you do not venture into the bay south of Cape Deveboynu. Some nautical books cite this well-protected, tiny bay as an anchorage, but it is in fact a military area, forbidden to private vessels.

JANCRIS sailed into this bay and a few seconds later, two military tenders full of armed personnel with automatic rifles came on board and ordered me to change course and head off immediately. We later dropped anchor close to the village of Eski Foça. We were rather frightened when this big Turkish Coast Guard motorboat boarded our ship. The military asked to see the ship's papers politely, and the transit log and passports. When they had made sure that everything was in order, the young man, who spoke English well, asked us why we were attempting to enter military waters so I showed him the nautical guide that reported anchorage without any restrictions. He then confirmed that many other yachts had come the same way, before starting up their powerful engines and moving slowly out into the open sea.

ILDIR (38°24'N 26°28'E)

The attractive Ildir Bay is forty miles away from Eski Foça. After the experience of the windy and rocky Cape Karaburun, you change course and sail southbound along the indented coast, to admire beautiful small and deserted beaches, which unfortunately are not hospitable to cruising vessels that anchor there. Better, sheltered anchorage, instead, is located on a bay on the southerly side of the village. If the sea and the wind are calm, then you can try the "one-boat anchorage" on the tiny islands of Karabag and Yassi. Unfortunately one nice anchorage, that of Karabag, is already host to a fish farm.

This corner of the Aegean Sea still preserves ancient Roman villa ruins just a few feet ashore.

Ildir anchorages are enjoyable if the meltemi is light. Don't miss a walk up to the acropolis before sunset, where you can enjoy a unique panoramic view and an absolute silence that bestows a peace not found in any city. You will remember the place for a long time.

CESME/SARPDERE

There are a couple of interesting anchorages if you have some days to spare sailing to Sigacik.

The first stop is in the lively little harbor of Cesme, a harbor that is well connected with the Greek island of Kios. A modern small marina is near the town, and the one named The Setur Cesme Marina forms part of a five-star hotel complex. It has a dock capacity for 180 vessels, full services available with electricity and water. A small yard can host 60 yachts ashore, courtesy of a sixty-ton slipway. Your second stop should be the forgotten bay of Sarpdere. You can try to anchor in the southerly desert cove, which is very narrow and only ten feet deep. For this reason you have to drop two anchors, the main on the bow, and the other, the stern anchor. But the work involved will be well repaid by a clean sea water and the beauty of the olive groves that cover the landscape.

www.seturmarinas.com

SIGACIK (38°11'.66N 26°46'.93E)

A large bay provides good shelter to an inner channel, which plays host to the all-weather natural harbor of Sigacik. If the meltemi is not blowing hard, it is possible to anchor before getting to the inner channel of the harbor, to benefit from more privacy and relaxation. You can swim from the boat in the clean, green water of the bay and feel refreshed. Once inside, you can berth under directions from the dock master of the Sigacik Municipal Marina.

In 2004, the municipal marina started work on enlarging the number of berths and providing more facilities to yachtsmen in transit. The sleepy town expands behind the public wharf, inside the high and well-preserved wall of the Genovese fortress that for centuries defended the low houses of Sigacik.

Port Facilities
To moor in this tranquil port, you have to drop the anchor in more than ten feet of water that has a dark, muddy, bottom that provides a good hold. Electricity and water are available on the dock, but the showers and the lavatory are insufficient for all the cruisers now visiting this village. The mooring fees are inexpensive, and you can pay directly the dockmaster who passes by late in the afternoon to collect the money. A small bazaar is situated close to the wharf, a perfect place to buy fresh fruit and tasty vegetables, and for those few spare dollars, there are more stalls with nice Turkish handicrafts.

Three fish restaurants are close to the dock, all similar, and the prices are fine. The open waterfront garden is occupied by the restaurants' candle-lit dining tables that illuminate the area and make for a charming atmosphere. Grilled grouper kebab is a specialty, as is "borek" with cheese, pleasantly swilled down with the local dry white wine. The best places, in my opinion, quality- and price-wise are Villa Doluca and Kavaklidere Cankaya. A normal fish dinner including a bottle of wine will never cost more than $30.

Not to be missed
Lying a few miles from the anchorage is the very interesting archaeological site of the ancient Greek city of Teos. This site has no impressive ruins, but imposing natural scenery. Luckily the recent construction of many ugly, white terraced houses is not visible from the site.

If the weather is calm and the forecast good, it is possible to go by boat and drop anchor at the foot of the cliff where Teos overlooks the Aegean Sea. The best spot for anchoring is in front of the small river mouth. On making your approach, watch out for two shoals that are not particularly easily seen because of the green, cloudy seawater.

KUSADASI (37°52'.1N 27°15'.6E POSITION OF THE KUSADASI MARINA)

Opposite the nice Greek island of Samos, along the Turkish coast, the wide bay of Kusadasi is home to the commercial harbor and the pontoons of Setur Marina. Approaching the bay, one can hardly escape the unsightly and uncontrolled developments that mar the coastline. Hotels, tourist villages, and terraced houses are built one upon another for miles. Luckily, in this expanse of the Aegean Sea with few coves or good anchorage, the bay holds little attraction for visiting pleasure boaters, with the only safe anchorage being in the marina. This is located in the heart of Kusadasi town and includes also a good yard with a large square. "Akburun Kayasi" is a shallow rocky reef that extends for five hundred feet in a westerly direction from the start of the outer marina's breakwaters.

Approaching the marina from the west, be aware of another rocky reef called Petroma Kayasi. This shallow rocky patch extends from Yilanci Burnu for half a mile in a westerly direction. The marina has mooring capacity for 350 yachts, and the yard has space for 175 boats.

Approaching the marina, you have to contact the Setur Marina office on VHF channel 73 or 16 and await the marina's dinghy to bring you in.

This marina is of particular interest because it represents the best and safest place for leaving the boat and seeing inland archaeological sites of exceptional beauty, such as Priene, Miletus, and Didymium with the marvelously preserved columns of the Temple of Apollo.

If you don't have much time, you ought to at least visit the well-known and unique Ephesus, only a few miles from the harbor. Getting to Ephesus is very cheap and easy thanks to the local buses called "dolmus," that do frequent daily trips from Kusadasi to Selçuk, the modern town nearest to this fascinating site.

The *dolmus* are the cheapest way to get about in Turkey, but for those who prefer it, an abundance of taxis can drive you anywhere—just negotiate the price first. Close to the marina's entrance, there is a taxi station where prices are on display in Turkish lira, euros and dollars for the most popular destinations shown on the billboard.

Before starting the journey to Ephesus, I suggest you go to the commercial harbor and see how many cruise ships are docked. Don't forget that each cruise ship puts hundreds and hundreds of people ashore, and in Kusadasi dock it is not unusual to see three of these floating cities on the water. Most of these people disembark just to go and visit Ephesus, so you can imagine the incredible crowds at a site like this. During the full summer season you can see up to nine cruise ships in the harbor. So, if you can wait, go to Ephesus when you see a maximum of two cruise ships there.

Port Facilities

Electricity and water are available in each berth, as well as mooring buoys and docking assistance. Fuel dock, a good number of clean lavatories with hot showers, a mini-market, wireless Internet connection, tennis courts and one swimming pool, a restaurant, bar, laundry, yacht chandlery, all inside the marina. The yard has an 80-ton travel-lift, and in the large square are all the shops to satisfy your sailing needs. Long-term storage is possible but in the winter season it is best to make an early reservation.

www.seturmarinas.com

Not to be missed

Top of the list is the archaeological site of Ephesus, and if you have time, the other sites of Priene, Miletus, and Didymium. The town of Kusadasi is nice and pleasant, even though crowded and chaotic when there are many cruise ships in the harbor. A walk along the bazaar street is an occasion to get some insight into the art of Turkish business. I say "art," because these people have an innate passion for commerce and business, and there is nowhere better to see it than in the bazaar. They have beautiful handicrafts, ceramics, carpets, jewels and clothes, and it is a beehive for tourists, with prices for all pockets.

Take a walk along the promenade connecting the marina to the city center—where many stalls sell pistachio nuts and other irresistible dried fruits and nuts—especially after sunset, when the sea breeze freshens the air and walking is so pleasant in this remote part of the eastern Mediterranean. Many restaurants catering to all tastes and pockets are located in the old city along the busiest streets. Here you can choose any dish you want, from juicy hamburgers to Chinese food or local dinners, without overspending.

ST PAUL'S PORT (37°39'.1N 27°00'.1E)

In the summer season, sailing from Kusadasi to this anchorage is normally a great day's sail, thanks to the meltemi blowing in a strong southerly direction in this area. Approaching the narrow channel that divides the Greek island of Samos from the Turkish coast, the winds can reach double the speed of those on the open sea. However, the wave motion is calm, and in such conditions, you can notch up record boat speed. A sailor's usual anchorage is between the tiny islands of Cil in the west, and Sy in the east. The mainland is northward. No more than three yachts can anchor in this small nook. Desolate and forgotten, this spot gives you the magical feeling of being the only people on the planet, particularly at night— after being surrounded by the deep darkness below deck, you can come up and be enchanted, admiring all the stars that light up the vaults of heaven. If the meltemi is blowing hard, on certain days, coming in to anchor you may be up against noisy backwash waves.

ASIN (37°16'.7N 27°34'.7E INNER CHANNEL PORT OF ASIN POSITION)

Approaching the beautiful moorage of Asin, you need not be put off by the hotel complex built on the western side of the inlet. It is better to face toward the inner channel of the small harbor. The entrance on the westerly side is marked by a Byzantine tower, while the easterly side is indicated by a simple pole set at the end of the old submerged breakwaters. The calm inner water is 12 feet deep and the sticky, muddy seabed gives you ample possibility to drop anchor and berth stern-to at the public wharf.

All you have to do is ask the dockmaster who is usually on hand to help tie you to the bollard and mooring ropes. He will charge you cheap mooring fees, and where possible connect the vessel up to the electricity supply and freshwater. If you need to refill a diesel tank, the dockmaster will summon a small tank truck to come to the wharf.

With the mooring operations finished, and time finally to relax, look around the deck and you will see a rare concentration of ancient ruins on the shore dating to different civilizations. The village of Kutin is composed of tiny stone houses, while on the surrounding hills, covered with olive trees, a medieval fortress overlooks the village and the bay. On an even higher hill, and after a nice, long stroll, you come to the ruins of Lassus, set in a peaceful, natural context. Be sure not to miss out on the small theater from which you can get an idyllic view. The peaceful anchorage and friendly inhabitants of the village leave you with happy memories of this harmonious spot. Onshore are a few grocery shops and handicraft shops, and several tiny taverns cook typical regional food at reasonable prices. If you have time and you missed out on the archaeological site of Ephesus, you can jump in a taxi from here.

YALIKAVAK (37°06'.4N 27°17'.5E)

Yalikavak is a tiny fishing village undergoing constant change and property development. The small port, cluttered with local fishing boats, boasts a new and well-equipped marina with travelift, supermarket and other facilities. Inland there are new buildings and some hotels built without spoiling the beauty of the place. Along the promenade you can find excellent restaurants serving up fish specialities at very good prices. Some shops and stalls sell carpets and handicrafts at bargain prices because there are fewer tourists here. There are very good road links thanks to the local buses already mentioned, which are efficient yet inexpensive. Electricity and drinking water are available directly on the dock. A small shipyard has technical staff on hand for woodwork, engine repairs, and jobs to be done in stainless steel. Here, too, a mooring fee applies. As an alternative to a port or marina, you can anchor in a northern inlet, but be ready for very strong meltemi winds coming down in gusts from the hills. The anchorage is comfortable, however, as the backwash doesn't come inside, and the seabed, which is a mixture of mud, sand and seaweed about 16 feet deep provides a very good hold.

Yalikavak is only 12 miles from the center of Bodrum, and 30 miles from Bodrum International Airport, while Dalaman International Airport lies 140 miles away, approximately the same distance from town as Izmir International Airport.

www.portbodrum.com

GUMUSLUK (37°03'.5N 27°13'.58E)

The small, quiet village is surrounded by the rather nice Gumusluk Bay, where low, stone houses, mixed with olive trees, in no way spoil the landscape of hills that overlook the bay. You can drop anchor there in up to thirty feet of water, but do not count on the soft muddy bottom for a good hold. In this village there are no services for yachts, just a jetty you can dock alongside. Be careful because the sea is no deeper than seven feet. Better to drop the anchor and berth stern-to the jetty's head. The village of Gumusluk is very well known in the region for its fish specialities. In fact, you will be surprised to see so many waterfront restaurants from the yacht in such a tiny bay. This nice fishing village is not, as yet, a tourist destination, so most of the restaurants' guests are local people who come here to enjoy themselves.

In any case, during the day the clear, calm water is irresistible, and a walk to see the ruins on the tiny island of Tavasan can be as good an excuse as any to go ashore. Another nice walk is to the bare promontory that offers good shelter on the inner water of the bay, overlooking a charming cobalt expanse of clean, glittering seawater. In addition there is the backdrop of the Greek islands of Leros and Kalimnos with their mountainous profiles. Ashore, late in the afternoon, most of the waterfront restaurants show a variety of recently caught fish, of any size and type found in the Mediterranean. After you have negotiated the price of your favorite, you can enjoy a great dinner with good service at a very reasonable price.

Sailing to Bodrum, just few miles from Gumusluk, you can see the high breakwater of the modern and full service Turgutreis Marina or D-Marin Yacht Club. This all-weather, well-protected marina can be a good alternative to the busy marina in Bodrum city.

For yachts from 27 to 50 feet in length, this marina has the finger piers system, while for bigger boats they use classic Mediterranean mooring. With a large square and a100-ton travelift near the marina, the yard can provide a full range of services.

www.dogusmarina.com.tr

BODRUM
See Part 1, page 50

GENERAL INFORMATION

Ideal for
Navigation is suitable for all cruisers interested in sailing to beautiful spots, where you can enjoy life on the boat in style, in tiny relaxing harbors with the full benefits of service marinas. If you aren't an expert sailor, is it is better to bring a local

skipper onboard because in summer, especially in July and August, the meltemi winds can blow strong for days, and can make navigation dangerous.

Weather
In wintertime, rainfall is abundant, while in summer it is rare, especially along the coast. The warm season is very long, and the best time to cruise is from April to the end of October. As already mentioned, the windier months are July and August, but June too, can be very windy. However, thanks to dry winds, the summer days are clear, and the colors of nature distinct and alive.

Reference Pilot Books
We sailed these waters using the *Turkish Waters and Cyprus Pilot*, by Rod Heikell, published by Imray.

Navigation Rules
There are no forbidden navigation areas. Entering and anchoring in the bays south of Eski Foça, Hacilar Limani is restricted, as is entering and anchoring on the small islands of Uzun and Hekim located ten miles south of Eski Foça Bay, in the Gulf of Izmir.

There is restricted entering and anchoring in the bay of Yenikale, five miles southerly from Izmir Harbor, but entry formalities are easy and quick to do by yourself or through an agent.

Connections
The city of Izmir and the city of Bodrum are well connected all year round thanks to their international airport and easy access by bus. Trips can be organized in the marina office to any destination by taxi or rental car. The roads are good, and outside of the big cities, the traffic is smooth and free flowing. The Greek islands of Kios and Samos are serviced daily by ferry connections, to the harbors of Izmir, Cesme and Kusadasi while Bodrum has several daily departures to the Greek island of Kos.

DISTANCES

Izmir – Eski Foça:	35 miles
Eski Foça – Ildir:	45 miles
Ildir – Sigacik:	55 miles
Sigacik – Kusadasi:	28 miles
Kusadasi – St Paul's Port:	13 miles
St Paul's Port – Asin:	35 miles
Asin – Yalikavak:	20 miles
Yalikavak – Gumusluk:	5 miles
Gumusluk – Bodrum:	17 miles

Index

Acknowledgments

Many thanks to my friend Giampietro Pini for his precious "freeze-frames" reproduced in this book at the beginning of each part. I can't give enough thanks to Michela Siviero, my umbilical cord on terra firma when I'm onboard JAN-CRIS. To Laura Fabiano, the translator of this book who now loves the Turkish Coast too, and thanks to all my friends who fill my life with human emotion and warmth. Lastly my darling Nicoletta.